PRAISE FOR THE GUILD
OF THE INFANT SAVIOUR

"The early life of an adopted child is mysterious, perhaps most of all to the child herself. In *The Guild of the Infant Saviour*, Megan Galbraith explores this mystery with delicacy and humorous intelligence, using science, art, and weird little dolls to guide her. What she finds is beautiful, sad, heartening, and mysterious. In its generous scope, Galbraith's book honors the depth and mystery of all human lives, whether we grew up with birth parents or not."

—Mary Gaitskill, author of *This Is Pleasure*

"An inventive, genre-defying look at what it means to belong. Galbraith artfully collects moments of her life and photographs from the past to create a touching portrait of motherhood, beauty, and home."

—Chelsea Hodson, author of *Tonight I'm Someone Else*

"*The Guild of the Infant Saviour* depicts adoption and motherhood with hard-won and clear-eyed pathos. Galbraith is a model observer; here life is set before readers like her photographs, arranged into beautiful and terrifying patterns that stand fixed in time but move in the mind."

—Matthew Salesses, author of
Disappear Doppelgänger Disappear

"An extraordinary collage of motherhood and a moving journey of one woman's search for wholeness. Megan Culhane Galbraith's personal story, braided with insightful research about adoption and foster care practices, and illustrated exquisitely with the author's photos, is a beautiful and memorable exploration of life."

—Jill McCorkle, best-selling author of *Hieroglyphics*

"This is the most ethereal yet earthly, dreamy yet disquieting book I have cradled, embraced, and, most importantly, *held*—an act made holy by Megan Culhane Galbraith. *The Guild of the Infant Saviour* is a book to be held and Megan Culhane Galbraith a voice to behold."

—Jenny Boully, author of *Betwixt-and-Between: Essays on the Writing Life*

"It's heartbreaking and fascinating to follow Megan Culhane Galbraith through the mysteries that make up this glorious, weird, tender, and revelatory book. Who are we? How did we become who we are? She knows these mysteries are unsolvable, but it is beautiful to watch her try."

—Ander Monson, author of *I Will Take the Answer*

THE GUILD OF THE INFANT SAVIOUR

MACHETE
Joy Castro, Series Editor

THE GUILD OF THE INFANT SAVIOUR

An Adopted Child's Memory Book

Megan Culhane Galbraith

MAD CREEK BOOKS, AN IMPRINT OF
THE OHIO STATE UNIVERSITY PRESS
COLUMBUS

Published by Mad Creek Books, an imprint of The Ohio State University Press.

Library of Congress Cataloging-in-Publication Data
Names: Galbraith, Megan Culhane, author.
Title: The Guild of the Infant Saviour : an adopted child's memory book / Megan Culhane Galbraith.
Other titles: Machete.
Description: Columbus : Mad Creek Books, an imprint of The Ohio State University Press, [2021] | Series: Machete | Summary: "A hybrid memoir-in-essays with photographs that confronts the realities of growing up as an adoptee born before Roe v. Wade, searching for birth records, examining the Domecon baby experiments, and interrogating the idea of traumatic memory itself"—Provided by publisher.
Identifiers: LCCN 2020049117 | ISBN 9780814257913 (paperback) | ISBN 0814257917 (paperback) | ISBN 9780814281192 (ebook) | ISBN 0814281192 (ebook)
Subjects: LCSH: Galbraith, Megan Culhane. | Adoptees—United States—Biography. | Adopted children—United States—Biography. | Birthmothers—Identification.
Classification: LCC HV874.82.G35 A3 2021 | DDC 362.734092 [B]—dc23
LC record available at https://lccn.loc.gov/2020049117

Cover design by Nathan Putens
Text design by Juliet Williams
Type set in Adobe ITC Galliard

For my children with all my love: J & J & S

An Adopted Child's Memory Book

CONTENTS

AUTHOR'S NOTE

The Guild of the Infant Saviour is a hybrid work of creative nonfiction. These are essays, prose poems, collage, photographs, and other experimental forms that use multiple artistic means to tell a story. It is part memoir, part social history, and part bedtime story. It is an interrogation of the very idea of memory. As such, it reflects the author's present recollections of recalled truth and experiences over time. All of the events depicted herein are true to the best of the author's memory. Some names and identifying features have been altered to protect the identity and privacy of certain parties, some events have been compressed, and some dialogue has been recreated. In relating the stories, events, dialogue, and scenes that the author was not present for, she has done her best to recreate them as they were told to her, and to remain true to the feelings and meaning of how they were relayed. The views expressed are solely those of the author. Dorothy Gallagher states it well: "Everything that happened is not in my stories; how could it be? Memory is selective, storytelling insists on itself." And as Tobias Wolff wrote in *This Boy's Life,* "This is a book of memory, and memory has its own story to tell. But I have done my best to make it tell a truthful story."

Little Megan

Prologue

Children play to control the world. When I was a child, I wanted to control my world because as an adoptee I felt I had no control. I created small universes populated by all sorts of figures: friends to have tea with, monsters to defeat, and new miniature realms to explore. It was empowering to make all the decisions, so I built dioramas and imagined myself into another life. It didn't matter that the stage was tiny. These were worlds into which I could disappear.

I'd just given birth to my first son when I found my birth mother, Ursula. I have changed her name to respect her request for privacy. I was twenty-nine years old. I learned she'd become pregnant with me and was sent away to a Catholic home for unwed mothers—The Guild of the Infant Saviour—in Manhattan.

Years later, I began playing with a tin dollhouse I'd found at a local antique shop; A '60s-era Louis Marx "Marxie Mansion" of the same time period in which Ursula was sent away to have me. I found a set of dolls from that era called The Campus Cuties. They were made from molded hard plastic like the toy soldiers of the time. I purchased some from eBay and then Etsy. The dolls had vacant stares and bullet bras like tiny, hyper-sexualized blank slates. Little girls had painted some of my favorites: their eyes black blobs; their clothing peeling off. I find them weirdly endearing. Their arms and legs are frozen in position and their names imply the roles society cast for women in the '50s and '60s—"Nighty Nite," "Lodge Girl," "Stormy Weather," "Dinner for Two," and "Shopping Anyone?" If The Campus Cuties were rendered in the flesh they'd have 40-inch inseams, 12-inch waists, and breasts the size of beach balls.

I hadn't been given dolls to play with as a child—no Barbie, or Baby Alive. I had no doll to feed, nor did I ever change a doll's diaper. Yet here I was a grown woman (a feminist!) besotted with these booby, leggy, plastic dolls. I was also in love with the tiny, delicate baby dolls. They too were made from plastic, although they were fragile as eggshells and the size of a three-month-old fetus. I collected them with obsessive zeal.

The dollhouse became a visual art project called *The Dollhouse*. I staged the Cuties and babies in household situations and photographed them from the outside looking in. I realized it was a voyeuristic way of seeing a situation from an angle of removal. It gave me the space I needed to examine my adopted life through a different lens. It emphasized a dystopia perhaps that was right there before my eyes.

I'd been the subject of many photographs—my dad being the photographer—but now, playing with these dolls, I realized I'd also been an object: a doll. Behind the lens of my camera, I am the director of my narrative. I've reclaimed a sense of control. Play calmed me down, allowed me to turn off my brain, and when I did, thoughts flooded in; memories returned. I became curiouser and curiouser. I began to ask uncomfortable questions. A window opened to a new way of seeing my reality.

Ursula and I have now known each other for nearly twenty-five years, and after hearing her tell me stories—shot through her lens of memory, grief, and trauma—I realize we have more in common than just the circumstance of my birth: we had both disappeared into our fantasies. Mine was tiny, imaginary, and voluntary; hers was all too real.

We'd both been pregnant with shame.

"No one gets a dollhouse to play at reality," said the child psychologist Erik Erickson, "but reality seeps in everywhere when we play."

As an adult, I see myself in early photographs and can identify the feeling of being fragile, helpless, and adrift. Like many adoptees, I've moved through depression, suicidal ideation, an eating disorder, anxiety, and sexual acting out. I've identified gashes of grief and shame: wounds I'd been licking instead of healing.

Adoption is what author Nancy Verrier called "the primal wound," and the resulting feelings of abandonment, shame, and loss are due to the severed connection between birth mother and child when a baby is taken away.

"Children are innocent before they are corrupted by adults," said Erickson, "although we know some of them are not and those children—the ones capable of arranging and rearranging the furniture and dolls in any dollhouse—are the most dangerous of all. Power and innocence together are explosive."

I realize now that I don't need to apologize for my existence.

The Dollhouse became a lens through which I could see my birth mother and myself. I could safely question my personal history and interrogate the myths of adoption, identity, feminism, and home. As an adopted child, I'd felt like a thing to be played with instead of a person with her own identity. I'd felt looked at, but not seen. I liked the idea of reclaiming what home meant to me by playing in my dollhouse because I'd never felt truly at home anywhere, not even in my own body.

Holding those fragile plastic babies in the palm of my hand made me realize I had to hold myself with the same delicacy.

Play helped me unlock ways of expressing the paradox of my identity as an adoptee while exploring intergenerational trauma, erasure, abandonment, and the myths and family lore that factor into many adoptees' origin stories. *The Dollhouse* photos in this book are recreating the original photos I curated from my Adopted Child's Memory Book, among other places. The original photos—like artifacts—appear at the end of each essay.

In *The Dollhouse* I created a world where women rule on a 1:12-scale: a portal to imagine myself into my birth mother's life and her into mine.

Our stories are fractured.

Our narratives double back on themselves like an ouroboros swallowing its tail.

Little Megan

Talking Points

Eve, the first woman on Earth, was created by God from Adam's rib. Is this where the phrase "he can't take a ribbing" comes from?

Divine rules were made to be broken.

Because she wanted knowledge and because the serpent suggested it, and because that crisp apple probably looked tasty, she bit it.

Then she shared a bite with Adam because she was *that* kind of girl. When God asked, Adam threw Eve under the bus. That was how she learned the difference between knowledge and wisdom.

She was warned. She was given an explanation. Nevertheless, she persisted.

Eve spelled backward is still Eve.

———

A 2014 poll reported that 56 percent of Americans believe that "Adam and Eve were real people," and 44 percent believe so with "strong or absolute certainty."

The story of Eve in the Book of Genesis is similar to the story of Pandora in Greek mythology.

In conceiving the world, Zeus asked Hephaestus to make Pandora out of earth and water.

Pandora was created as a punishment for all mankind.

In mistranslations of the origin myth, Pandora's clay jar became a box. Both are metaphors for the uterus.

In the myth, Pandora opened her box filled with curses from her angry dad-god Zeus and out came death, pain, promiscuity, disease, lies, misery, secrets, greed, narcissism, envy, loneliness, jealousy, fury, and passion.

Is this where the concept of "Daddy issues" comes from?

Hope remained under the rim of the jar.

Hope in a Jar is a brand name of a skin cream that sells for $22 per ounce.

Hope was the 146th most popular baby name for a girl in the year 2000; its popularity has now dropped by 50 percent.

———

"Box" is slang for lady parts: a metaphor for the uterus and vagina.

Other words with metaphorical meaning for "something that holds or contains" include: chalice, grail, jar, urn.

I read that ancient Egyptians interred their fetuses and children in clay jars which, when excavated and cracked open, resembled womb-like eggs.

I think of these vessels, and I think of Pandora, a woman formed from clay—a mortal woman of the earth.

I think of Eve, mother of all the living, condemned to eternal pain in childbirth because of that one sinful bite.

———

When I first met my birth mother, she told me how good she was at giving blowjobs. She said she couldn't understand why a woman on her knees gave men such a feeling of power. "If you think about it," she said, "you could just bite it off."

———

Before the 1850s the American public did not consider a fetus to be a person or abortion to be a crime.

As I'm writing this, pro-life groups continue to assert that life is created at the moment of conception.

The Catholic Church owns one-sixth of the hospitals in America and operates ten of the twenty-five largest health-care networks.

I was treated once at a hospital called St. Mary's. The first thing the intake nurse asked me was if I was prepared to take the Lord Jesus Christ as my savior.

My children are not baptized.

In 2009, five women nearly died from prolonged and traumatic miscarriages because the Catholic Hospital, Mercy Health Partners, had a strict ban on abortion.

The definition of mercy is: "compassion or forgiveness shown toward someone whom it is within one's power to punish or harm."

The March for Life's 2014 theme was "Adoption: A Noble Decision." Many pro-life groups use the term *pro-adoption*, but I am not their poster child.

————

An ancestor of mine invented the paperboard box by accident, and with it ushered in the advent of modern packaging.

A former male boss of mine said of a colleague—a "problematic woman," in his words—that he was able to just "put her in a box" by giving her menial tasks of no consequence.

Another male boss proclaimed daily that we all needed to think "outside the box."

I once worked in a cubicle for five years.

When investigators finally discovered H. H. Holmes, the country's first-known serial killer, they found, among other things, a wooden box containing several female skeletons. He intended to sell them to a medical school.

In the nineteenth century, illegitimate children were viewed as evidence of wrongdoing and illicit sexuality. Foundling hospitals left boxes on their doorsteps, into which "fallen women" placed their babies.

In 2017, news broke that a nearly hundred-year-old mass grave was excavated in Galway, Ireland, beneath the Bon Secours Mother and Baby Home. The remains of nearly eight hundred babies and children were found in a septic tank.

An "accident" is a euphemism for an unwanted pregnancy.

As an adoptee, I think a lot about the difference between a mistake and an accident.

————

Being adopted feels sometimes like being reborn from a clay pot, or being formed from the earth, or from a man's rib, or from anger, or as a punishment.

Oedipus was adopted. So were Moses, Hercules, and Romulus and Remus. They were all abandoned by their birth fathers. They were all fucking mad about it. They were mythical men who started a lot of wars.

I'm unsure who my birth father is. My birth mother told me his name, but she also said, "It was the '60s, it could have been anyone."

Other famous adoptees include: Richard Burton, Babe Ruth, Bill Clinton, Edgar Allan Poe, Frances McDormand, John Lennon, Jamie Foxx, Marilyn Monroe, and Malcolm X.

———

I continually try on identities and feel like an actor in my own personal theater productions of *The Good Child* or *Don't Ever Leave Me Again* or *See, I Am Worthy of [insert here: Love, Kindness, Joy, Pleasure]*.

We mythologize our narratives to better explain the world to ourselves, perhaps to suit the story to the Self.

I loved to listen to the stories my birth mother told me—and how she embroidered my origin. But memory is malleable. The act of remembering is always remembering.

———

In *Ways of Seeing,* John Berger wrote: "Men look at women. Women watch themselves being looked at."

The Madonna and Child is one of the most popular and recognizable images in the world, and therefore the most looked at.

I recently saw the Della Robbia exhibit at the National Gallery and lost count of the terracotta versions of the Madonna and Child I saw.

The Italian term *terra cotta* means "cooked earth."

I felt gutted recently, looking at a friend's photographs of the earthly places where young women were killed or last seen. Drug addicts, prostitutes, "she lived a high-risk lifestyle," "she was asking for it," "she was in the wrong place." Theirs is a shallow grave of erasure. They were someone else's children.

How do you witness invisibility? How do you listen into a silence?

My therapist, in trying to give me tools to console myself, suggested that I imagine myself as a child, "Little Megan."

"Hold her," she said, "hold her as you would hold your own children." It made me gag with tears.

I've looked a lot at the Madonna and Child. I see them differently now.

———

Other names for Mary are: Blessed Mother, Our Lady, Madonna, Mother of God, the Virgin, the Magdalene.

In the Gospel of Luke, the angel Gabriel visits the Virgin Mary and tells her she will conceive and bear a child. He says that the Holy Spirit will "come upon her" and that "nothing will be impossible with God."

My middle name is Gabriella; originally given to me by my birth mother as my first name before she surrendered me for adoption. My adoptive father believes that the nuns named me for the archangel Gabriel.

Before my birth mother was sent away to The Guild of the Infant Saviour, her parents met with who they thought were my birth father's parents. They called her a "slut" and a "whore."

Sigmund Freud wrote, "Where such men love they have no desire and where they desire they cannot love." This is called the Madonna-Whore complex.

I fantasize about being fucked from behind, with another man's cock in my mouth. Call me a dirty whore if you want.

———

At camp one summer, all the girls were reading Judy Blume's book *Forever*. I couldn't understand how the teenaged boy could "come inside" the main character, Katherine. I was confused by the use of the verb "to come," and was too afraid to ask the other girls about it. To me, it was as if the boy had opened a portal inside the girl and invited himself in.

———

In all these stories, the woman is the receptor, the chalice, the jar, the grail. She is molded from, come into, killed, cleaved, boxed and sold, imbued with the evils of the world. Her origin story is a paradox.

She is set upon the earth to be both gazed upon yet reviled; to imperil and seduce; to be made impure and discarded—a slut, a whore.

I cannot unsee this. I cannot look away.

————

I experiment with agency, pushing into something before shamefully walking back my desire. I'm trying to abandon the box I've neatly packed myself in.

I think about gathering up the love I feel for others and sending it to myself, just to feel hopeful about opening it.

Pack, unpack, repeat.

Forward-side-together. Backward-side-together. The Box Step is a dance.

————

On Valentine's Day 2017, a Republican representative from Oklahoma, Justin (J. J.) Humphrey, introduced House Bill 1441. The bill specifies that women get written permission from a fetus' father before obtaining an abortion. He said:

> *I understand that they [women] feel like that is their body. I feel like it is separate—what I call them is, is you're a "host." And you know when you enter into a relationship you're going to be that* host *and so, you know, if you pre-know that, then take all precautions and don't get pregnant.*

Emily Virgin, a fellow Oklahoma State Representative, called the language "incredibly disrespectful."

In biology, a "host" is defined as "an organism that harbors a parasite and supplies it with nutrients. The host does not benefit and is sometimes harmed by the association."

According to the 2010 census, only one in ten children live in a family where the father is present.

Myths become misinformation become entrenched belief systems.

Forward-side-together. Backward-side-together. This dance is always the same.

She was warned. She was given an explanation. Nevertheless, she persisted.

She was born to bear it.

Pregnant Pause

The Hoosick Falls, New York, Grange Hall smelled of hay chaff and linoleum scuffed with stale cigarettes. We sat on plastic folding chairs around bridge tables under fluorescent lighting, rising to assemble cold-cut sandwiches and accept limp pasta salad doled out from aluminum baking trays by the gossip-tongued ladies' auxiliary. It wasn't the kind of baby shower I would have planned for myself, but it was the one I'd been invited to.

I know rural towns. I grew up in one. Now, my husband and I lived five miles from Hoosick Falls (pop. 3,400), in the rented first floor of a dilapidated nineteenth-century farmhouse down the road from where Grandma Moses was discovered. In Hoosick Falls, 4-H groups met in barns to practice clipping cows for the county fair. It was real 4-H, not the prissy stuff I'd learned growing up in rural, privileged Connecticut, like how to balance a teacup and saucer properly on my lap. Although we'd had cows growing up—and turkeys, and sheep, geese and a horse—this place felt a world apart.

Joyce sat at the front of the room and opened her gifts—crocheted pink blankets; pink and yellow onesies; baby's tiny first shoes. Like me, she'd been adopted and had never met her birth mother. But Joyce knew more about her origins than I did. She'd lived in this little Upstate New York village her entire life. Joyce was aware that her birth mother still lived in town. As far as she knew, they'd never encountered each other.

We had talked about how strange it would have been for Joyce to run into her birth mother on the street. "What if she goes to your church?" I said. "How do you know she isn't a teacher at your kids' school?" But she was content with her life and ambivalent about wanting to know the woman. I told her I would have found it hard not to scan the faces of women on the street or in the grocery store for signs of familiarity. Now that I was pregnant myself, I suddenly needed to know everything I could find out about my birth and my birth mother. Pregnancy intensified everything for me. My hair was thicker, my skin luminous, and my ankles swollen. What if my birth mother had felt the same things? What if she'd felt my first kick, like I'd felt my child's first kick, and fell so in love (as I had) that the idea of surrendering me was greater than the idea of dying? That's how I felt about the baby in my belly, and it made me want to know her story all the more.

———

Earlier that day I had received a thin envelope in the mail. It was from Catholic Charities in Bridgeport, Connecticut—the agency that coordinated my adoption nearly three decades earlier. There were mysteries no one volunteered to help me solve. I wanted answers.

For as long as I could remember, I'd only had a passing curiosity about my birth mother, but becoming pregnant changed that. The baby's hold on me was firm, immediate, and visceral. For the first time, I began to put myself in my birth mother's shoes. I imagined giving my child to another woman, making her a mother. My questions shifted from how hard it must have been to relinquish me, to simply "why?" Why had she surrendered me? Or had she abandoned me? It was impossible to imagine letting my baby go. It would have been like losing a limb and having to live with the ghost pain forever.

I was chronicling our life in a diary for my first son called "Letters for Tomorrow," a baby shower gift from one of my closest friends. I'd do the same for my second son. "I hope this will allow me some closure," I wrote about beginning the search. "I hope it will answer some questions."

―――――

The envelope from Catholic Charities had arrived moments before I walked out the door for Joyce's baby shower. I left it on my nightstand, unopened. Here I was, pregnant myself, celebrating another woman's pregnancy while possible answers about the mystery of my origin waited for me at home. The irony nagged at me as I ate pasta salad and watched Joyce open her gifts. I knew the envelope held my "non-identifying information," the paperwork my birth mother (or her mother, or the caseworker) had filled out when she'd been admitted to the The Guild of the Infant Saviour. But what would it say?

It was hard to imagine what my birth mother may have been feeling when she filled out those forms. I had no starting point from which to calibrate my thinking, no touchstone. She could have been in her early teens, pregnant after her first sexual experience, or forty and burdened with too many children already. How would I untangle, for my children, the genealogical Gordian knot of a mother and a birth mother? My caseworker told me that the information provided could be rich or spare, truth or lie, depending upon who filled out the forms. In many cases it was the birth mother's mother who completed the intake papers. If that was the case, she explained, sometimes they obfuscated facts or didn't provide any in order to remain untraceable.

As I'd waited for the envelope to arrive, I ran through the possible scenarios as I lay in bed with my husband. "Was I wanted or unwanted? A mistake or an accident? Should I request more information, or should I leave it alone? Did she marry my father? If not, who was he? What would you do?"

He answered through closed eyes, "I would go to sleep."

———

The caseworker said that many birth mothers during the late '60s were in fear when they came to Catholic Charities. There was shame, she said, and there was usually an angry or concerned mother sitting nearby, worrying them to "put this behind you, and get on with your life."

Here I was, married less than six months and pregnant much sooner than I'd expected. I also had a worried mother to contend with.

When I'd called Mom to tell her I was pregnant, she'd fallen quiet on the phone. "Aren't you happy for me?" I asked.

"Of course I am," she said. "I just thought you'd wait a little bit, so you and Jeff could spend some time together by yourselves."

———

My baby was about five months into gestation, and I was beginning to show, though everyone said they couldn't tell I was pregnant and I could cover my belly with a loose cardigan. I wondered if my birth mother had felt me wiggling deep inside her belly. What it had meant to her. Had I been a welcome twinge? A harbinger? Maybe she just thought she was gassy? Now, at the shower, I squirmed uncomfortably and shifted my legs under me, pushing my folding chair back from the table. So many thoughts were flying around in my head and I couldn't talk about them. It didn't help that the small talk from my mother-in-law, Lois, was rapid-fire and full of judgment.

"I had Paul on our kitchen table," she said, pushing the food around on her paper plate, separating the tuna fish from each pasta spiral with her plastic fork in jerky stabbing motions, like her right hand was having little seizures.

"These days having babies is so complicated, what with the C-sections and the Lamaze and all the machines and the drugs," she went on, nodding in my direction without looking up. "You people don't even have to worry about the pain anymore."

Lois rarely called me by my name, addressed me directly, or even looked at me. She used the phrase "you people" most often about Jeff and me: "What are 'you people' doing for summer vacation?" or "What are 'your people's' plans for Christmas?" Her inability to embrace me as her daughter-in-law felt like another maternal betrayal. I'd been hopeful about having another mother figure, perhaps a supportive one, but it wasn't in the cards with Lois even if I was carrying her grandchild.

I disliked her immensely.

———

At the front of the room, Joyce was slowly pulling ribbons through a flimsy paper plate she'd adorned with the adhesive bows from her gifts.

"It's a "bow-kay," said Lois, throwing her head back in a laugh. Joyce heaved herself up from her chair and pointed to a pine dresser that had been hand-painted with a Disney scene of Bambi, Thumper, and Flower.

"Donny done that," she said, referring to her brother. "He done it himself."

———

I smelled the Chock full o'Nuts percolating in the Grange Hall's kitchen. I looked around at the mothers, daughters, and children assembled there. My mom was in Williamsburg, Virginia, and my extended family was scattered across the country. I wondered who would throw me a baby shower. Were these my people now?

I felt trapped in a country-fried noir film.

———

Jeff and I had been married for less than a year and we were working jobs with a combined income of about $20,000 when I got pregnant.

Nearly three months to the day I'd stopped taking the pill, I was standing in the aisle at the Bennington, Vermont, Rite Aid comparing accuracy rates on off-brand pregnancy tests. I could sense I was pregnant. It was as though a light had flickered on in my belly—as if a tiny ball bearing of an oracle was rolling around inside me.

It made me wonder how and when my birth mother knew she was pregnant. Back in the '60s they didn't have over-the-counter pregnancy tests. Had she missed her period? Had she had terrible morning sickness? Had her breasts swelled? Was her hair lustrous and thick, like mine?

I bought the Rite-Aid brand dipstick-style test and drove home. I peeled off the plastic wrapping and held the white stick under the warm stream of my urine, dousing my thumb. I rested the test on the back of the toilet and washed my hands. The bright blue line emerged through the heart graphic, indicating I was pregnant, and all I could think was, *holy shit*. I was terrified. It was real. What was I going to do? I was an adopted person who didn't know her ancestry. I was a person who didn't know her people. I felt suddenly irresponsible for bringing a child into the world without knowing my heritage. I worried that all the stories and family lore I'd be passing along were adjacent ones, not biological, not the truth—like these narratives were mine, yet not mine. It was as if I were two people and had parallel life somewhere else.

What were the stories I'd be telling my children? What was the truth?

————

Lois was wearing a sweatshirt she had bought at a craft fair. It was maroon and decorated around the neck with puff-painted flowers and a lace Peter Pan collar. Her earrings were sterling silver, accented with turquoise and coral. She reminded anyone who would listen that she was one-tenth Cherokee. Those were her proud people. Much later, her son would take a genealogy test and not find a drop of Native blood; no one had the heart to tell her.

Sitting on that uncomfortable folding chair, I wondered about my people. Would my birth mother resemble my crass, judgmental mother-in-law, or my loving but sometimes distant adoptive mother? Would I like her? Would I hate her? Would I even want to meet her? Would she look like me, talk like me? Would she want to meet me? Had I ruined her life back then? Would I ruin her life (again)?

"Is that where 'you people' are having your baby?" Lois asked under the buzzing fluorescent lights. She was looking over my head as she spoke as if trying to find the daughter- in-law she had always wanted—the one who loved endless chitchat and shared her interest in hand-decorated sweatshirts and Yankee Trails bus trips to The Mall of America.

I hadn't wanted to share with her that I was hoping to have the baby in one of the new water-birth tubs at Albany Medical Center, or that we were trying to choose between the Bradley Method and Lamaze class, or that we had opted for a midwife instead of the OB/GYN. She wouldn't have respected those choices. Not because they were unfamiliar to her, but because they were mine.

———

The Catholic Charities caseworker had spoken bluntly about what the envelope might, or might not, contain. Now that I had the non-identifying information, I would have to make hard choices. I might open that envelope and find out things that could unravel me. What if my birth mother had been raped? What if she was destitute and wanted to come live with us? What if I had brothers and sisters? What if she was dead, and I couldn't get answers to any of my questions?

If I tried to contact my birth mother, would I be inviting someone else's demons into our life? Pursuing further information was my decision, the caseworker said. I had full control of the process. As the next step, I could request a ten-hour search for her, or I could do nothing. But how could I decide when I didn't know the full consequences of my actions? How could I move forward with a fraction of the story?

I wanted to hear my birth mother's story firsthand. I wanted to bond with her. I needed to find the ghosts of my past in order to place myself within some biological context. Maybe knowing my birth mother would make me a better mother. Perhaps it would help me understand things about my personality that hadn't meshed with my adoptive parents. Meeting her could provide me a sense of ease with myself, like looking deep into my own eyes in the mirror.

Or maybe, what I didn't know could never hurt me.

———

I pictured the envelope lying on my nightstand. I thought about opening it carefully, with the idea of preserving each moment and not tearing the envelope or the papers inside in my haste to gain access to my information. I imagined giving myself a paper cut as I slid the sheets out of the envelope.

I looked around the Grange Hall, trying to route a mental map of my departure through the phalanx of relatives and Joyce's friends. How would I get out of there quickly, without getting pulled into helping in the kitchen, or having lengthy small talk, or stuffing gifts into the trunk of Joyce's mom's Impala? I wanted to get home and back to that envelope.

———

Overhead, the fluorescent lighting cast a vanilla glow. I heard chairs being pushed back hard against the linoleum. It was time to leave.

Back home, I found the envelope where I had left it on the nightstand next to my bed. I crossed my legs under me on top of my grandmother's hand-stitched quilt. I turned the envelope over, unfastened the brass clasp, and slid the papers out.

I felt the baby bear down on my bladder. I took a deep breath.

———

She was nineteen when she gave birth to me. I'd lost my virginity when I was nineteen.

She was a Scorpio with brown hair, green/blue eyes, and fair/freckled skin. I'm a Scorpio with brown hair, green/blue eyes, and fair/freckled skin.

On the pages, in her halting and nearly unintelligible penmanship, I was struck by how much I identified with her. Even her handwriting resembled mine.

TALENTS, HOBBIES, SPECIAL INTERESTS
very organized
good singing voice
interest in the arts, dancing (ballet + modern)
acting, writing poetry, reading

FUTURE ASPIRATIONS
To be a magazine editor

———

It is incredible how few concrete details I needed to feel connected across time. We shared a mutual love of books, music, and dance. I'd begged my parents to let me play the violin beginning in fourth grade. I'd danced with The Royal Academy of Dance up until high school, written poetry, fiction, and essays, and spent so much time reading in solitude that my adoptive mother once asked, "Honey, don't you want to go outside and play?"

On my father's side, she'd listed no age, just that he was Caucasian and English. He was more than six feet tall with blue eyes, blond hair, and fair skin. In the sections for his interests and aspirations she noted:

TALENTS, HOBBIES, INTERESTS: ?
FUTURE ASPIRATIONS: ?

———

I began to think about who I was at nineteen—a virgin for starters—and how incomprehensible it would have been to become a mother when my own future felt like it was just beginning.

———

MANNER IN WHICH PLANS FOR THE CHILD'S FUTURE WERE MADE BY THE PARENTS. REASONS FOR CHILD BEING PLACED FOR ADOPTION:

*Since the birth mother is unwed, she is receiving
no support from the birth father and thinks it best
for the child to be adopted by a stable, loving family
to best offer the child all the advantages she is unable
to give.*

———

She didn't receive prenatal care until she was five months pregnant according to the paperwork. And he was no saint, but she also seemed forthright and unashamed.

———

DRUGS TAKEN DURING PREGNANCY

Alcohol:	AMOUNT: an occasional beer	HOW OFTEN: once/twice a week
Marijuana:	WHEN: first 4–5 months	AMOUNT: total about 1 oz.
Cigarettes:	WHEN: throughout	AMOUNT: 10–15/daily

———

She'd updated the paperwork within the last ten years. Her mother, my grandmother, had taken a drug called Diethylstilbestrol (DES) during her pregnancy. DES was a synthetic form of estrogen given to women between 1940 and 1971 to prevent miscarriage. The daughters of women who used DES were forty times more likely to develop cancers of the cervix and vagina.

Medical terminology deemed them "DES Daughters."

The drug's side effects were known to skip a generation, meaning, they may have affected me—or worse my unborn child. Late-onset and irregular periods were one side effect for DES granddaughters like me. I didn't get my period until I was sixteen: my biological mother got hers at around eleven. Other risks included infertility, cancer, congenital disabilities, and "fewer live births."

I worked myself into a frenzy about this. I called my doctor; I demanded they double-check the health of my baby. I went to the library and researched the effects and side effects of DES. After I'd calmed myself, what struck me most was that my birth mother had cared enough to update my file.

One of my biggest fears about finding her was that she wouldn't want to be found. But here she'd left a medical clue in these papers that signaled she was thinking about me. She'd left a Hansel and Gretel-like trail of bread-crumbs through the woods, as if willing me to find her.

So I did.

The Guild of the Infant Saviour (circa 1940).
Photo courtesy of New York City Municipal Archives.

Sin Will Find You Out

"My water broke late in the afternoon, around rush hour on Lexington Avenue," Ursula said.

When I met my birth mother it was 1996, and I was twenty-nine years old; she was just shy of fifty. Ursula had rented a room at the Manhattan Fitzpatrick Hotel in Midtown. She said she wanted to "show me around the neighborhood," which is why we were a few blocks from the Guild of the Infant Saviour, the Catholic unwed mothers' home where she spent four months leading up to my birth. I had just given birth to my first son and that weekend marked the first time I had been away from him.

Ursula told me about the day I was born.

"I was trying to hail a cab with my 'baby buddy,'" she said.

I imagined two teenaged girls, both swollen and pregnant, one waddling to the curb and waving a frantic arm for a cab while my birth mother's water rolled down between her thighs and into her shoes.

"We had no contact with anybody, no family contact, nobody," Ursula said. "That was a rule."

———

The Guild of the Infant Saviour was located on East 52nd Street between First and Second Avenues. Ursula's parents sent her to live there when she couldn't hide her pregnant belly anymore. She told me she had been keeping the pregnancy secret as best she could, but at five months the borrowed girdles and large sweatshirts couldn't hide her growing bump.

"Call us when you have the baby, and we'll send you money for a ticket home," her mother had said at the train station, before shoving a one-way ticket into her hand.

———

Years later I would search for photos of what the Guild had looked like, but I would find only one from New York City's Municipal Archives—a photo from the 1940s, taken for tax purposes, showing a pair of mid-nineteenth century Italianate brownstones missing their stoops. In the photo, they stood like widows holding hands. The window shades were drawn—as though the entire place had its eyes half closed. Along with its triplet next door, made prettier by the grandly swooping front staircase, the buildings formed a quiet facade on a normal Manhattan street. About twenty unwed mothers were living at the Guild when Ursula was there with me in 1966.

"I remember smells and boredom," Ursula said. "We sat around waiting for our babies to be born. No joy in the waiting because we knew we were giving them up. Everybody smoked like chimneys. We sat in a dismal cloud of smoke in the living room on some old couches watching a black and white TV."

I imagined the girls perched like fat robins on musty, donated sofas. They did their laundry, made their meals, and cleaned. I could almost smell the cigarette smoke and Lysol. Changing the channel probably meant heaving themselves up to flip through television shows, adjust the rabbit ears, or tune the three channels that marked their tedious days.

A typical Monday of TV watching in 1966 may have been like this:

Morning: *I Love Lucy, Supermarket Sweep, The Dating Game, Father Knows Best*
Afternoon*: As the World Turns, General Hospital, You Don't Say, The Match Game*
Evening: *Bonanza, I've Got a Secret, My Three Sons, Bewitched, I Dream of Jeannie*

Ursula told me the nuns rarely let the girls out of the Guild by themselves. The few times Ursula convinced them to let her go out alone, she walked to the Central Park Zoo, sat on a bench, and smoked cigarettes for hours, watching the penguins glide silently underwater.

———

Ursula and I smoked cigarettes, drank red wine, and traded stories like we were old friends. In between stories I used my Medela breast pump. I was committed to nursing my first son, who was at home with my husband—I was horrified with myself for drinking and smoking while I pumped, but that didn't stop me. Ursula told me that my middle name, Gabriella, was the one she had given me at birth.

"My dad thought the nuns named me for the archangel Gabriel," I said.

"Actually, I named you after Gabrielle 'Coco' Chanel, a feminist icon of mine," Ursula said. "I must have been reading her biography at the time. I had a notebook of names for my future kids. I think Megan was one of those names, but there was also Daisy, Gabriella, Amanda, Calliope, Ariadne—the Greek goddess who untangled the spider's web, or maybe it was the Gordian knot." When she said, "The nuns were my first feminist icons," I nearly choked on my wine.

She gasped when she realized I had grown up less than two miles from her childhood home in Norwalk, Connecticut. "My mother played bridge with your grandmother!" she said, slapping her knee and lighting another cigarette.

Ursula told me we were Hungarian and that we were related somehow to Bela Lugosi, who, she remembered, pressed a quarter into the palm of her hand at a family function.

I had brought my pink Adopted Child's Memory Book to show Ursula photos of me as a little girl. She marveled at the sterling silver baby gifts from Tiffany my mother had listed in her careful cursive handwriting.

"My mother would have been so proud to know you were adopted into a better social class," she said, exhaling smoke around her head.

I was confused. Why would Ursula's mother care what social class I belonged to when she didn't want me to begin with? I realize now that this was just the beginning of the stories that would never add up, of falsehoods disguised as fact, and of memory as a coping mechanism. Back then, though, I was simply searching every inch of Ursula's face for some sign of family resemblance.

We walked around the neighborhood, and she showed me where the Guild had been. The facade had been redone years ago and housed the Hungarian Consulate; its red, white, and green flag whipped and snapped overhead.

Ursula told me she didn't sign away her parental rights until I was about six months old. She said she tried to keep me and visited frequently, "signing me out" and "trying to make a go of it with me herself." She said that the '60s weren't a good time for someone trying to be a single mother living in New York City.

When has it been a good time to be a single mother? I thought.

———

Years later, after I had done more research through Catholic Charities, the agency that facilitated my adoption, I would find out that I had spent the first five months of my life in a foster home in New Fairfield, Connecticut. It was nearly two hours from New York City. My legs were in braces that were supposed to heal my hips from dysplasia. The caseworker at Catholic Charities who was helping me with my research told me they had hoped this would ensure I wouldn't limp. It seemed doubtful that Ursula could even have made that kind of journey to visit me—it was a two-hour train ride, plus a bus, from New York City—much less bring me back to her apartment and try to "make a go of it."

"It feels strange to tell you this," said the caseworker, "but you would have been considered a special needs child back in the '60s."

If my legs hadn't healed—if I had limped—the chances of me being "unadoptable" were high. If that had been the case, she told me, I could have spent my life in an institution. But I did heal, and I was placed in a lovely home, even though I had to wear the braces on my legs when I slept.

My adoptive mom and dad had been vetted and selected by the caseworkers, and I would meet them for the first time at the Catholic Charities offices in Bridgeport, Connecticut.

"The caseworkers brought you there with me to say goodbye," Ursula said, "but I wouldn't sign, and there was a huge thing about that, so they all went out into another room to talk about it. There was this huge pile of papers on the desk. I flipped through them and was convinced you were with some family named Starro in East Lyme, Connecticut. I remember them bringing you back in. 'Don't get attached,' they said. 'Don't get attached.'"

Ursula said her mother came into the room and told her, "You sign. Or, you know, that's it." So Ursula said she signed the papers.

Later, in the room where the adoption was formalized, Ursula said she watched the proceedings from behind a one-way mirror. My adoptive parents had arrived after Ursula signed the papers. They did not meet each other. Mom, Dad, and I were now a family: we were on the other side.

———

The girls at the Guild had all given birth at a charity hospital in Hell's Kitchen called St. Clare's. It was located on 51st Street between 9th and 10th Avenues. I wanted to visit the places Ursula had been, so I went to the hospital where I was born.

Founded in 1934, St. Clare's Hospital was a healing crossroads for artists, indigents, and the working classes of Manhattan. In the late 1980s, New York State and federal health officials designated it as the first comprehensive AIDS center in the country—the largest hospital at the time (250 beds) to be devoted to the treatment of AIDS. But in the 1990s, time was running out for the hospital. It was too small, too antiquated, and too expensive to operate. The Archdiocese merged St. Clare's with St. Vincent's in Greenwich Village, and the decline accelerated. The hospital ceased operation in 2007.

When I got there in 2009, it was abandoned. Squatters were living there, the windows were boarded up, and the doors were chained together. I thought hard about squeezing through one of the broken doors. I wanted to know what the maternity ward looked like. I wanted to see it with adult eyes and stand in a spot that might allow me to feel an umbilical connection to my flesh and blood. When I shared this idea with Ursula, she told me I was crazy. I asked her to remember it for me.

"I remember a big rectangular room with eight metal beds—four on each side—and a linoleum floor, a crucifix over each bed, and the chart hanging from the end of the bed," she said. "There were no distinguishing features except a big window at the end. The nursery was down the hall—big picture windows with lots of newborns lined up with pink or blue knitted caps."

Over the original transom that bears its chiseled name—St. Clare's Hospital—was a life-sized cement statue of St. Clare of Assisi holding a chubby infant in the crook of her left arm. She hovered, barefoot, above the faded blue awning like a forgotten Madonna.

"My labor was long, about sixteen hours, and about the worst pain I remember," Ursula said. "It was like shitting a watermelon. If anybody ever had a second baby, I could not tell you why. I don't know how anyone would go through it again.

"I was in that clinic with every doctor on earth up to his elbow down there," she said. "I was like the practice dummy. And I said originally that I didn't want any drugs to the guy that helped me through the labor—his name was Dr. Moon, he was Korean—and then I kept saying 'Dr. Moon, give me those drugs,' and he'd say, 'Now, now, you said you didn't want any drugs so just breathe.' I was in a labor room with four beds, one occupied by a Puerto Rican woman who was yelling her head off. I remember asking the nurse if there was something they could do to help her. The nurse told her to 'offer up' the pain and 'God would reward her with a wonderful baby.'"

They were both wheeled into the delivery rooms at about the same time.

"I remember someone saying, 'This one is nine fifteen, and the other is nine twenty-five.' And I remember saying, 'Wow! No wonder she was screaming, a nine-pound, twenty-five-ounce baby. That's big!' That's how out of it I was."

During Ursula's delivery, she told me, the doctor performed three episiotomies—one on each side and one up the back. As she told me this, I chanted silently: *Father, Son, Holy Spirit*. I imagined many of the Guild girls carried these same scars.

I remembered the birth of my son, who was delivered by emergency C-section. My doctor held him up for me to see and said, "Judging by the size of his head, I think you're lucky it worked out this way." It made me wonder about the trauma Ursula may have gone through having me (with my own generously sized head). I wondered if she would have had a C-section had we not been a charity case.

The papers listing the details of my birth showed that I had been a high forceps delivery. It was the kind of delivery that resulted from the baby being under stress. It also resulted in extreme tearing and trauma to the mother. By today's standards, it may have been a routine C-section to reduce the risk to mother and baby. A forceps delivery can trigger a type of facial palsy in the baby, causing the child's mouth to droop on one side. This explained the sneer I have lived with my entire life, the one that enticed the boys on the school bus to call me "Sidecar," a jeering name that stuck with me throughout high school.

In the mid '60s birth control for most women was mechanical and meant condoms or a diaphragm. Abortion was illegal, and although the pill was available in many states, it was a crime in Connecticut to use any form of birth control due to Comstock Laws that prohibited use of "any drug, medicinal article or instrument for the purpose of preventing conception." This was overturned in 1965 by the US Supreme Court case—*Griswold v. Connecticut*, 381 U.S. 479—in which the Court ruled that the Constitution of the United States protects the liberty of married couples to buy and use contraceptives without government restriction.

My birth father, according to Ursula, had joined the Navy. "His parents called me a slut," she said. That word stung me just to hear it. They challenged her parents to prove it was their son's baby. I remember gasping audibly when Ursula told me, but she waved it off like she was made of Teflon.

"When you were born I called my mother and told her I had a daughter," Ursula said. "She wanted to have nothing to do with it. That was it. One day you were there, the next day you were gone."

The Guild girls were not allowed back after they had their babies at St. Clare's. Ursula spent five days in the hospital and then took the train, alone, back to her parents' house in Norwalk, Connecticut.

"Depending on circumstances, I guess you went back where you came from," she said. "I imagine that many girls were picked up by their parents."

Her borrowed maternity clothes, "all raggy things," were returned to the Guild by the hospital, laundered by the remaining unwed mothers and placed in a "found box" for incoming mothers. They even recycled underwear, she told me.

I was born four years before Governor Rockefeller legalized abortion in New York State.

————

I began retracing Ursula's steps by visiting the places in New York City where she went when she was pregnant with me. I thought it might provide me solace, or give me a sense of where I had come from. I drove by the house where she grew up in East Norwalk, Connecticut. It was a modestly sized, nondescript tract house in the Strawberry Hill neighborhood across from Devine's Dairy Farm, which was owned by my adopted father's cousin. My dad spent summers helping out on that farm.

Ursula's childhood home was little more than a mile from the home I was adopted into. Did that happen by design? I wondered. Had I known, I could have walked to her house as a child.

Most of these places as she knew them are gone now, surrendered to the march of time. St. Clare's is now high-end apartments; the Guild has been absorbed into three buildings that house the Hungarian Consulate; and Ursula's childhood house is home to another family.

These places haunt my dreams. There has been no sense of closing the circle, or of finding answers. These places are pieces of my history that have vanished, leaving nothing but a vapor trail.

———

At dusk, I walked east on 51st Street toward 8th Avenue and away from the now abandoned St. Clare's Hospital. In the distance, getting closer with each footfall, I saw a ten-foot-high neon cross. The sign—a landmark in the city—hummed on and off. As I got closer it flickered its message: "Get Right with God."

I stopped for a minute. I smelled scuffed gum on the sidewalk, faint body odor pollinated the air, and I could feel neighborhood eyes on me. I watched the red and white sign unfold its message across the darkening sky. I kept walking and turned back to look up at the other side, which was now fully lit.

It read, "Sin Will Find You Out."

Ursula graduates from St. Bernard's School, Pittsburgh

New York Is Beautiful STOP
Love, Elizabeth Caldwell STOP

This narrative is stitched together from letters and journals given to me by my birth mother. It involves both our voices which blend and embellish each other.

When my parents told us we were moving from Pittsburgh to Germany, that's when I knew I had to run away. I was born for Pittsburgh. I could go anywhere; get anywhere. I owned that city and I was only thirteen years old.

In the summer I hung out at the local swimming pool, where I pretty much went every day, all day. I also took ballet lessons twice or three times a week. I loved it and took the streetcar downtown by myself to school—I went to Saint Bernard School and Miss Maddy, the teacher, drove me home. We lived in a rented house in a suburb city of Pittsburgh.

I spent my middle school years there, had a lot of friends and a lot of freedom to roam the neighborhood and the city because of public transportation and, I guess, my age. I was pretty mature for my age.

I had so much freedom. I knew the bus routes and the drivers and could get anywhere I wanted. It was a gritty, smoky city full of sound and the smell of huge factories gaping and yawning in the heavy winds where the Three Rivers came together. In Pittsburgh, I had places to hide, to be alone, to think.

I loved St. Bernard's. It was as Catholic as it comes . . . uniform, knee socks, Black Watch plaid or navy jumper, pleated skirt, culottes or slacks. I was popular, had a lot of friends, and it was academically challenging, something I had not had since leaving Connecticut. After the intellectual wasteland of rural Georgia (where we'd lived previously) my mother was keen to explore the city, so we went to museums, galleries, libraries, conservatories, lectures, took advantage of all that Pittsburgh had to offer. It was very interesting and alive for me: new life, new people, new ideas, new experiences.

By the time I graduated eighth grade, I could have easily been mistaken for nineteen or twenty years old. I was tall and quite developed in my St. Bernard sweater with a well-defined waist. I was feeling all-around quite womanly on the outside, but I was still a kid. I played jokes on Daddy, like the time on April Fool's Day I replaced the sugar with salt. He was roaring laughing. My mom, after that first sip of coffee, went into a rage and sent me to my room.

If Mom only knew what I did in the afternoon. She didn't care as long as it didn't affect whatever she did during the day. Daddy worked in the steel mills back then. Mom would shove my sisters and me out of the house on weekend mornings with just a peanut butter sandwich. "Don't come back until dinnertime," she'd yell out the door. We had no idea how she spent her day: smoking, cleaning, or watching her stories, possibly. She had aspirations, dreams, and maybe she worried they would never be fulfilled in this "stinking, rotting, old town." My dad was in the Army and we moved quite a few places in my childhood: Norwalk, Connecticut, until I was nine, then Columbus, Ohio, Georgia, Pittsburgh, so when Daddy told me we were moving to Germany I had to make the first move.

One day I got into my mother's closet, dressed up in her clothes and went and bought myself an airline ticket to New York City. I was 13. I just acted as if I knew what I was doing and it worked.

The only person I told was my friend Greg. I told him I was running away and would let him know I was safe by sending a postcard or a telegram from New York City signed Elizabeth Caldwell, the name I had fashioned for myself to keep the subterfuge alive. I was quite heady with the entire idea of escaping my old life for the life I had always imagined: being free and living in New York City. I imagined I would be a magazine editor, a fashion writer, or a dancer. I would live in a beautiful, small apartment all on my own, one that I furnished from the thrift shops. I would date musicians who smoked and played in the dirty bars in Greenwich Village, the ones you got to by going downstairs. And I would find girlfriends who shared my intellect—no stupid-mongers for me—I knew what I wanted to be in life. Nothing was going to slow me down, especially going to Germany. I cared not one bit about that place. I didn't know anyone; I didn't care to know anyone; I told my parents, "I. Won't. Go."

Fighting with my mother was useless; she would dig in her heels and there was no talking about anything. It. Is. Done. Well, we'll see. She couldn't keep me a prisoner and I was thirteen and if I didn't want to go with them, I was perfectly capable of living on my own.

I flew TWA into Idlewild Airport in New York City. From the air, the landed planes looked like delicate dragonflies. From the tarmac, the TWA terminal resembled a huge white seagull, poised for take-off on the macadam. In the terminal, on the TWA red carpet, I was surrounded by glass and concrete that swooped up and curved around me. I saw a few military men/boys pacing in camouflage and a lot of glamorous women with their hair freshly set, wearing pearls, pumps, and fur, carrying miniature suitcases that I assume held their cosmetics.

I must have taken a taxi to Grand Central Station, though I don't remember how I got there. I sent a Western Union Telegram to Greg from Grand Central. It said:

NEW YORK IS BEAUTIFUL STOP
LOVE, ELIZABETH CALDWELL STOP

I picked that alias from a movie or a book of that time and now can't remember which one or what the significance was.

Then I took a train to East Norwalk, Connecticut, where Grandad was waiting at the station, apparently having met every train that had come that day. My parents must have called ahead to him because when the train rolled to a stop, there he was waiting for me on the platform.

Mother was furious and ordered me to stay right where I was. I knew my mother let me stay in Connecticut as a way of letting the steam build up for our reunion. In the meantime, she packed everything I had for our move to Augsburg, Germany (I called it Ughsburg).

As a teenager, I "developed" early and had very big tits, which attracted quite a lot of boys, but a big mouth to match, which scared them away. I remember having a lot of boyfriends, but not many real dates. In retrospect, most of those boys were probably gay and are "out" (the closet was very large and dark in those days) and loved me for my spirit and humour (sic). I was a good and generous friend.

I started to go bad (as my mother would say) just before we moved to Germany and got worse when living there. This was probably because I was no longer intellectually challenged (Army schools or life were not high on intellect) and my parents had a new baby. Oh, and probably because I also discovered beer and the BOQ (Bachelor Officer Quarters) and started to drive. I managed to get through freshman and sophomore year at Augsburg American High School, but was starting to get too friendly with the second lieutenants (no one would believe that I was just 15) and was shunted off to the Salesian Convent of Saint John Bosco in Limerick, Ireland, for my junior (and final) year. There, although feeling greatly abandoned, cut off, and hard done by, I had the luxury of my personal nun tutor and not only managed to pull off an unprecedented seven "A" levels in the British General Certificate of Education (GCE), but to get almost perfect scores on my SATs and hence early admission to college.

I could have gone to Bennington, Wellesley, or Sarah Lawrence, or even Manhattanville, but my parents chose Ladycliff College in Highland Falls, New York, because it was run by nuns and was next door to West Point where I could get free medical care and use the PX (the Post Exchange was like a department store just for military families). I lasted a year; did well academically, but discovered sex and got caught out after curfew and in trouble for smoking in my room. I broke about a million other rules and was asked not to come back.

My parents were still in Germany and I was living with my grandparents during the holidays. I then spent a semester at UConn before giving up and getting a job.

It all gets a bit hazy then . . . it was 1966. That was the year you were born.

Permission not granted

You on your nap mat

Find Me Here

Monica is my best friend, and she has agreed to accompany me on my research trip to the New York Public Library's genealogy section to search for my birth mother. We are bumping downtown from Columbia University on the A-train.

It's the late nineties, and I am newly married and a few months pregnant. I don't yet know that I can simply pick up the phone and request a search for my birth mother through Catholic Charities. All I have at this point is the number from my adoption birth certificate—it appears in the right-hand corner—36369. My adoptive birth certificate includes the fact that I was born in Manhattan, New York, but lacks valuable information such as my height, weight, hair, and eye color. Back then; I naively thought adoptee data was stored in one place, and that by going to that place it might be possible to find the details of my birth, even my original name, and my birth mother's. That place, in my mind, was the genealogy wing of the New York Public Library.

I went in search of my self.

"I see her being a famous magazine editor," Monica said, swinging herself around by the crook of her elbow on the shiny chrome pole of the subway car.

"What if she's homeless? Or in a mental institution?" I said. "Or what if she's penniless and wants to come live with me?"

"She's probably pretty musical since you are," Monica said.

"I just found out Joni Mitchell put a daughter up for adoption and is searching for her now," I said. "Maybe I'm Joni's daughter, wouldn't that rock?"

"You're like an honest-to-goodness love child," Monica laughed.

"Or the by-product of rape," I said.

————

The Irma and Paul Milstein Division of United States History, Local History, and Genealogy is huge and airy. It smells of leather-bound books, oak, and old paper. The librarian is behind a sleek oak desk, and filigreed iron staircases lead up to the stacks.

"Do you have your number on your birth certificate?" she asked. I volunteer the slip of paper.

"Oh, I don't need it, but you will," she said. "Do you know the last name of the person you want to look up?"

"Last name?" I said. "No, that's kind of why I'm here."

"All our records are alphabetical by birth year," she said, looking over her glasses. I feel my heart begin to palpitate. Monica sees the rising panic on my face.

"I'm sure you have an alphabetical cross-reference, right," I said. "You would think, but no," she said.

I begin mentally haranguing myself. I'd thought the search for my birth mother would be natural. I'd thought a simple number would unlock all the clues, like a codex, or the keys to a safe deposit box full of family secrets: as if this library full of information owed me something. As if by possessing this tiny data point, I could access my entire biological life story that would rush into my brain and make me feel whole, and right, and real.

"Come on," Monica said. "How hard can this be? You said you think you're Irish, so I'll take the 'O's for like, O'Connor, O'Hearn, and O'Malley and you start with the 'C's' for, I don't know, Cavanaugh, Connelly, and names like that."

I didn't know what or who to think I was. Whose identity could I claim? How would I begin to guess where to start looking? My adoptive parents were Irish and Polish, but that meant nothing in the search for my true identity.

"Alright, let's do this," I said.

The librarian climbed down from her perch, crossed the floor and ascended another set of stairs. She emerged with four black-bound volumes the size of her torso. They looked as if they held ancient spells.

We find an empty table and sit down on the hard wooden chairs. I open one of the books to a random page. I see columns of arbitrary numbers on the left—the numbers I need to match with mine. The columns go on for volumes, and the paper is tissue-thin. The information is single-spaced, in 12-point, Courier type, and—just as the librarian had indicated, it is in alphabetical order by last name. I have a number, but no name. I feel like I am an adoption Catch-22; needing to know my identity before I can find myself.

Monica and I spend the better part of the day tracing row upon row of faceless, numbered columns. She has a brilliant idea to handwrite my number on the blank side of an index card so we can trace the edge of each column without our eyes crossing. We find amalgams of the number. Each of us rises halfway out of our chairs with excitement, only to realize we have transposed one or two digits—36396 or 36936. It feels like a demented genealogical lottery. By late afternoon, I am exhausted, have a headache, and feel guilty about dragging my friend into the mess of my unknown history. Finally, when we feel it has been enough for one day, we leave the index cards on the floor and ride the subway back to Harlem.

Five years later, I find out after meeting my birth mother that I wasn't the by-product of rape, or incest, or even a one-night stand. I was either an accident or a mistake, although what's the difference? If the timing had been different, I suppose I could have been an abortion.

A few years after meeting Ursula, I returned to the New York Public Library. The long oak tables, brightened by huge windows that let in the light off 5th Avenue, are littered with people's laptops and iPods.

I still have my number, but this time I also have a name. I want to see if I can find myself among the books now that I know where to look.

This is how I am listed in the 'H' book titled, "BIRTHS Reported in the City of New York, 1966:"

NAME, LAST/FIRST	DOB	BOROUGH	NUMBER
Herman, Gabriella	10 XX 66	M (for Manhattan)	36369

I gasp. I know my middle name was the name given to me at birth, yet seeing it in writing makes it real and no longer simply a romantic story. I will later find out that no nuns ever cared for me. Instead, in the five months between my birth and adoption, Catholic caseworkers, nurses, and an Italian foster mother cared for me.

I felt cleaved. I had two stories, two full identities. I felt apart—other—from both of them. Yet for one moment, in searching for myself, it turns out I had been here all along.

You on your nap mat.
Courtesy of Michael B. Culhane.

My children: Jenna, Jesse, and Sam, 1997.
To whom this book is dedicated.

What to Expect When
You Least Expect It

A monitor beeped, and I heard my midwife Robin say "C-section" again before it registered. There would be no pushing, no birthing tub or mixtape, no aromatherapy candle. "I'll be right back," she said. When she came in the next time, she had Dr. Clarke, my OB/GYN, by her side. He was already in his scrubs. It wasn't even 9 a.m., and already I was a lousy mother.

Dr. Clarke was a barrel-chested bald man, standing about six-foot-three, with a left-side comb-over. His handlebar mustache was waxed up into a smile, and his scrub mask nestled under his chin.

Robin patted my forearm. "Everything will be fine."

But I wasn't fine. I hadn't slept well the night before and had spent it staring at the ceiling making a mental list of the things I didn't have ready yet for this baby: onesies, stamina, cloth diapers, motherly tendencies, blankets, surplus love to share, warm sleepers, unselfishness, a job. I had been expecting for more than nine months; surely by now I should have known what to expect.

My husband, Jeff, and I skipped the last Lamaze class altogether. "I can't believe they're ending class on the C-section," I said to Jeff. "It seems so negative. Besides, look at me," I said, making palm parentheses on each side of my ample hips and shrugging my shoulders. "This baby is going to squirt out like it did for that Catholic woman doing dishes at the sink in Monty Python's *The Meaning of Life*."

I had planned to give birth with no pain medication in the new birthing tub that had just been installed at Albany Medical Center. My first-born would come out swimming like a tadpole, and I would be blissed out in the warm water, forgetting any pain or bloody afterbirth floating around like ship wreckage. In the week after my last OB/GYN appointment, I made Jeff drive me over bumpy backcountry roads to induce labor on my own terms. I swallowed capsules of evening primrose oil and drank raspberry herbal tea. And we had sex. Twice. My cervix didn't dilate a centimeter.

We had talked about giving birth at home. At the time, Jeff and I were living in what my family called "the abandoned farmhouse" in Eagle Bridge, New York. It was Grandma Moses country. She lived, painted and was discovered a half-mile away. We were so remote and rural that a friend standing on our front porch said, "Well, it's not the middle of nowhere, but you can certainly see it from your house."

The three-story white clapboard farmhouse, replete with widow's peak and a ghost, peered over the abandoned Eagle Bridge passenger railroad station. Cargo and freight trains ran through twice a day, and when they stopped and idled for hours in the middle of the night, the engines shook every pane of glass. I could feel the vibration of the idling train as I lay in bed or sat on the couch watching TV. Once I got used to the sound, it helped me sleep. It also masked the skittering of squirrels, mice, and pigeons in the uninhabited upstairs.

We loved that farmhouse. Its floors sloped and buck-led; the two closets were the size of a thimble. In the win-ter I'd sit on the couch with my legs crossed and watch mice run laps around the living room. When the heater couldn't keep up in the 30-below weather of that first winter, the wide-pine floorboards shrunk their seams a quarter-inch and I could see down into the dirt basement.

"Are you going to bring a baby into that cold house?" Mom said.

"What are we going to do Mom, leave it at the hospi-tal?" I said.

My mom called every day after my due date to check up on me. This was years before everyone had cell phones. At the time I was hauling home salvageable fur-niture from local tag sales and repurposing it for the baby's room, which meant a lot of sitting on the floor and painting. When the phone rang, I had to heave my-self to my knees first, grab a chair, and pull myself up to stand before waddling to the kitchen where the phone was attached to the wall.

"How's progress?" Mom said.

"Get this kid out of me!" I said. "I go to the doc-tor this week for another checkup. The midwife said they wouldn't let me go beyond ten days. I just don't want that pitocin."

"I worry about a baby in that cold house."

"I know, Ma, I know."

I began doubting my due date and my midwife. Had she miscalculated? I started to suspect that this baby was never coming out. Even the train arrived and left on somewhat of a schedule.

"Don't move," said the anesthesiologist. I tried yoga breathing—in through the nose, out through the mouth—as I hunched over on the operating table holding Robin's hands. I remember them being warm and strong. She wore a ring on her left hand: an oval sapphire surrounded by tiny diamonds. She was petite and had a sturdy jaw that dared me not to trust her. Her eyes were kind and as blue as that sapphire.

My hands were shaking. I could smell antiseptic and iodine. These were not the smells I had hoped would accompany my first child into the world. I felt so cold. "The operating rooms are kept cold," Robin was telling me, but I didn't listen to the reason why. I was trying to take my mind off what was going on behind me. I was anticipating the anticipation of pain. I was expecting to be a paraplegic or bleeding to death on the operating table or the baby strangling on the umbilical cord. I thought I was prepared. I felt pressure, I felt a little sting, and then I felt warmth flood my pelvis from the epidural.

Robin's hand was between my shoulder blades, and she helped me lie down. I realized I couldn't use my stomach muscles. My entire torso was now shaking. She covered my chest and arms with a warm, thin flannel blanket. I relaxed a little while the epidural paralyzed me from my armpits to my toes. The feeling of the narrow surgical table on my back faded away.

The nurses strapped my chest and torso down with Velcro belts and splayed my arms out on separate little tables, fastening them with Velcro as well. I felt like Jesus on the cross, except with tubes and needles and a blood pressure cuff squeezing my right bicep and making my hand numb.

My husband shuffled in the operating room in blue disposable surgical coveralls. "Stylish," I said. "Do you get to keep those?" He had on the same puffy scrub cap and booties to match everyone in the room. The nurse clipped a sheet to the steel frame at my torso so I couldn't see the procedure. Then she reached up and flicked the overhead surgical light on, pulling the red handle into place for the doctor. It was a mirror-like umbrella that focused the light beam on my belly. To my horrified curiosity I realized that I could watch the action in its reflection. I felt disembodied like I was dead and alive at the same time watching the entire cesarean from above.

"This is what it must be like to be awake during your own autopsy," I said.

Someone was talking to me, but I couldn't make out who it was behind the blue masks. I couldn't see anyone's mouth moving.

"This is a teaching hospital, and students learn by watching these procedures," a doctor said. "Do we have your permission to allow medical students studying OB/GYN to observe your procedure?"

Seriously? I remember thinking. Seriously? You strap me down, nearly paralyze me, dress my husband in crazy pants, and now you're going to ask me if people can watch?

"Whatever," I said.

"Are you right-handed or left-handed?" the nurse asked. "What's that got to do with anything?" I said.

The nurse held a clipboard with a form in front of my face.

"Right," I said. She put a pen in my right hand and held the clipboard in front of my strapped-down arm. "Any way you can take that blood pressure thingy off my finger?"

No sooner had I signed the paper than about fifteen med students shuffled into the O.R. and formed a semi-circle around my feet and behind the doctor.

Dr. Clarke asked, "Can you feel this?"

"Feel what?" I asked.

"Ok, we're ready to begin."

In my head, I was yelling "Wait, hold on! I'm not ready!" I didn't think this would all happen so fast, me getting pregnant within the same year we got married. I wasn't entirely sure I wanted kids just yet. I didn't understand what it meant to have them or not. I was still processing that I even had a choice in the matter.

I held Jeff's big, rough hand. It was the hand of a dairy farmer and the man I loved: The father of my baby, a good father to his nine-year-old daughter—my stepdaughter. His hand was warm when mine was cold, steady when mine was shaking. I looked at him, breathed, and relinquished what has always been hardest for me to give up: control.

I could sense the doctor rooting around, and I could hear everything he said. "Prep the area. Iodine. Scalpel. Now I'm going to make a series of incisions, first through the layer of subcutaneous fat. Do you see that?" Was he saying this for my sake or for the medical interns who were standing around my feet? "Now I cut through the fascia, and you'll see the abdominal muscles. Scissors. Be careful not to cut the bowel or the bladder . . . ."

I began wisecracking: "While you're in there can you do a tummy tuck?" I said.

"Dr. Clark, have I ever told you that you remind me of my high school Latin teacher? I feel like I should be singing some Gregorian chant right now."

By now he was pushing his gloved hands inside me, and I could see my lower body moving back and forth on the table as though he was loosening the baby's grip on my ribs.

"He's really going at it," I said to Robin. "Am I going to fall off the table?"

I kept glancing up into that mirrored light. If I concentrated on the outermost rim, I could look right down on the action. My skin was white and curled back in wrinkles at the sliced edges. It was pulled open by stainless steel clamps. I could see my fat, yellow and bubbly, and my blood was bright red in some spots and brownish yellow in others. I looked away. I looked at my husband. "I'm cold," I said.

"The baby is coming," Dr. Clark said to my husband. "If you'd like to watch, you can stand up and look now, but only if you have a strong stomach."

"It's okay," Jeff said. "I've seen this done with cows hundreds of times." I gave him a look. "Thanks a lot," I said.

"You know what I mean," he said.

In the time it took to look away from the overhead lamp and see my husband rise to peer over the blue sheet, I heard the tiny cry.

"It's a boy," Dr. Clarke announced, using a bulb to suck the juice out of the baby's lungs and nose. "A healthy boy. He's beautiful." He cradled Jesse for me to see. The umbilical cord was still attached, like a gray extension cord running from me to him. In Dr. Clark's enormous blue-gloved hands Jesse looked like a large red kidney bean with his toothless mouth fashioned into a bawling "O." His eyes squinted against the bright light. I worried he was cold. The nurses wrapped him in a flannel blanket and went about their job of weighing and APGAR testing.

"Bring him over here. Bring him here. Untie my arms." I pleaded.

I kept my eyes on those nurses: they weren't switching my baby at birth. Then, Jesse was safely in my husband's arms. His hands, reddish-pink, smooth, warm and new, were miniature replicas of my own. His fingernails were translucent as waxed paper and his little knuckles un-puckered and pulled tight as he grabbed my finger and wrapped his tiny hand around it.

I didn't care what the doctor was doing to me now even though I could sense him plying the afterbirth out of me with his backhoe hands. The gawking med students disappeared. I felt warm.

My son was holding my finger.

My children: Jenna, Jesse, and Sam,
1997. To whom this book is dedicated.
Courtesy of the author.

Image	RT-AB-35
Year	1921
Topic	Resident Teaching > Apartment Babies
Text	June 5, 1921. "Here shown in the arms of his 'Mother of the Day', Elizabeth Cooper Baker, '21. Dickie came to us a little nothing baby and graduated after his ten month stay with a fine vocabulary of one word, which he used eloquently, enthusiastically and efficiently – "damn."

Dickie Domecon

Hold Me Like a Baby

Their names were Dicky, Dickey, Dickie, and Donny. There was Bobby, Bobby II, Bobbie III, Grace, Edna Mae, and Joan. They were also called "Apartment Babies," or "Practice Babies," and they shared a last name—Domecon; short for Domestic Economics.

Plucked from local orphanages, asylums, and almshouses, hundreds of these babies were chosen to help college coeds "apprentice for motherhood."

In 1919, Cornell pioneered the first degree-granting program in the country for women called "Domestic Economics." Its aim was to apply scientific principles to domestic tasks deemed "Mothercraft"—such as making meals, cleaning and ironing, household budgeting, and raising children. Female coeds—five or six at a time—lived together in on-campus "Homemaking Apartments" and collectively mothered the practice babies.

Ranging in age from three weeks to a few months old, babies were loaned to the college for a year. The contracts between the orphanages and Cornell stated the babies "could be returned at any time if there was dissatisfaction on the part of the college."

Their birth names and identities were erased, and they were fatted and raised by a rotating lineup of up to six practice mothers at a time. The co-eds' work was divided into six parts, including the job of mother and assistant mother.

Domecon babies were highly sought-after for adoption. Adoptive parents were convinced that because the babies were being raised in ideal conditions and by scientific methods it would ensure a smooth family transition. A 1923 newspaper article titled "Coeds at Cornell Mother Real, Live Practice Babies" referred to the babies as "super children."

The program ran through 1954. In all, 119 children were raised in this manner and adopted, and Dickie Domecon was the first. Most grew up with no knowledge of having been abandoned or surrendered, or having been a Domecon baby.

All identifying records were destroyed.

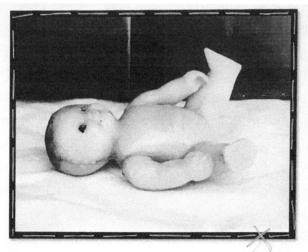

Image   RT-AB-39
Year   unknown
Topic   Resident Teaching > Apartment Babies
Text   Dicky; 1st Home Economics baby.

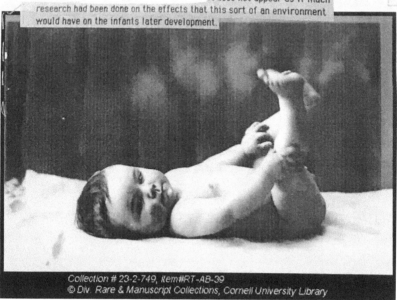

it does not appear as if much research had been done on the effects that this sort of an environment would have on the infants later development.

Not much research has been done on the effects.
Courtesy of Div. of Rare & Manuscript Collections, Cornell University.

———

Three stories underground in Cornell University's Olin Library is the Carl A. Kroch Library, home to the Division of Rare and Manuscript Collections. Built in 1992, the bright finishes—skylights, white paint, light oak, and a soaring atrium—are the opposite of dark or musty, as I've come to think of an archive. The surroundings seem counterintuitive to the trip back in time I am planning to take.

Gaining access to the Domecon records was easy and the process felt oddly sanitized. The librarian walked me through the computerized system and printed me a ticket; I handed it to the archivist and waited at one of ten tables in the reading room. As I waited, I wondered how many others had inquired about the program in general and the babies, specifically. As an adoptee, I know the feeling of wanting someone to come looking for me. I also know that being found can feel like opening Pandora's box.

I'd come to Ithaca on a month-long writing fellowship at The Saltonstall Foundation. It was the first time I'd had the luxury of time to spend with my art and away from the stresses of everyday life. It was a solitude I was unused to. I'd become frustrated with my work and myself. I complained to a mentor by email that the hard work of writing about traumatic subjects felt like I was "sitting in my own poopy diaper." She'd replied, "That's exactly how it's supposed to feel." An outing to the library seemed just the thing to get me out of my head. I figured I'd find some books to read, take a walk, and pull myself out of my funk. I don't remember the string of words I plugged into the library search engine to arrive at the information about the Domecon babies, but down the rabbit hole I went.

Back at the reading room table, I watched as a staff person carried in a stack of four archival boxes. Inside were carefully labeled folders with photos, ephemera, and student papers printed on dot matrix printers, along with various pamphlets and civic duty bulletins.

I spent days hunched over the table pawing through the material. It seemed the focus was on programmatic aspects of the then cutting-edge degree and its pioneering feminist leaders—Martha Van Rensselaer and Flora Rose—rather than on the babies, who seemed to have been treated like interchangeable laboratory specimens and less like tiny humans. All that remained of the 119 Domecon practice babies were a few dozen photographs.

The black and white photos showed college co-eds vacuuming, preparing baby bottles, diapering babies, and generally practicing at motherhood. In the photographs taken of the babies themselves some were chubby and exuberant, others emaciated and sickly. All of them were posed, propped up, and no doubt encouraged to smile. It seemed to me to be the commodification and idealization of what a "real child" should be: plump and happy: a confident blank slate.

I took iPhone photos of as many photographs as I could and returned to my studio where I recreated the scenes in the '60s-era dollhouse I'd brought with me. I'd found more of the fragile plastic baby dolls at a local junk shop that were similar to the two I'd brought with me and used them as stand-ins for the practice babies. A toy company called Renwal manufactured the dolls in the '50s and '60s. I could fit four of them in the palm of my hand.

I realized later that I was conducting my own experiment. I was playing with the concepts of home and family. My baby dolls were objects of play, but the Domecon babies were real experiments: human objects. Recreating their photographs in the dollhouse made the practice of practice babies seem dystopian.

———

By the time I was born in 1966 and adopted in 1967, Second Wave Feminism was in full-throated, radical, and revolutionary mode. The National Organization for Women (NOW) was founded in 1966 by Betty Friedan and twenty-eight women with the purpose to "take action to bring women into full participation in the mainstream of American society now, exercising all privileges and responsibilities thereof in true equal partnership with men."

But the difference between the political rhetoric and what was taking place on the ground for women was vast. Activists protested for equal rights, equal pay, and equality, yet here I was in utero with my birth mother who'd been sent away in secret to have me. Homes for unwed mothers, mostly white women, thrived through the mid 1970s. It was still considered a family burden and a shame to be unwed and pregnant. Abortion hadn't yet been legalized in 1966. In Connecticut, where my birth mother lived, any form of contraception was illegal for unmarried women until 1972.

Conservative opponents to feminist principles, like Phyllis Schlafly, proclaimed, "What I am defending is the real rights of women. A woman should have the right to be in the home as a wife and mother."

It all sounded very 1919.

After she'd given birth to me, Ursula told me she'd stayed in New York and worked in publishing as an assistant. She'd been fired from a job for wearing a pantsuit and had lived in what she called "the girl ghetto," an apartment she shared with other young, single, working women, on the Lower East Side.

"Women have babies and men provide the support," said Schlafly, "If you don't like the way we're made you can take it up with God."

———

Because I'd spent my first five months in a foster home, in leg braces designed to heal hip dysplasia, I likely wasn't picked up much, or comforted when I cried. I've spent years, and hours of therapy, trying to unravel the complex emotions that come from what my therapist deemed "mild attachment disorder," which the Diagnostic and Statistical Manual (DSM 5) describes as, among other things, ". . . a problematic pattern of developmentally inappropriate moods, social behaviors, and relationships due to a failure in forming normal healthy attachments with primary caregivers in early childhood."

"I always wondered about that flat spot on the back of your head," my adopted mother said to me once as she stood at the counter preparing dinner. "I don't think you were picked up much as a baby."

I imagined myself as an infant; chubby thighs pinned wide with a metal rod thanks to a hip abductor brace. Had they not healed correctly, I'd have limped or had my legs permanently braced, my caseworker said. I'd have been unadoptable and likely institutionalized. Back in those days, she said, "No one wanted to adopt a baby with a deformity."

As a child (before I knew any of this information), I'd convinced myself that one leg was slightly shorter than the other. I'd worried I had a limp that no one was acknowledging for fear of making me feel different. I felt different deep in my bones. Sure, I looked like my parents—I was white with brown hair and they were as well—but I felt othered. That I couldn't see myself in my parents' faces created a void. As I dug into my research with the Domecon babies and the contracts that contained the clause about babies being returned, I realized my unconscious fear of being returned as a child to the foster home. I began to understand how being adopted fostered my deep insecurity, distrust, and fear of abandonment.

————

I had three mothers before I was six months old: my birth mother, my foster mother, and my adoptive mother.

————

Image   RT-AB-30
Circa   1935-1936
Topic   Resident Teaching > Apartment Babies
Text   Rose Ann and Mary Alice, twin practice babies. No date given, but
they were here around 1935-1936.

Rose Ann and Mary Alice.
Courtesy of Div. of Rare & Manuscript Collections, Cornell University.

———

The science of child rearing in the '60s—in fact, throughout history—demonized mothers for everything from making their children homosexual to being the cause of their sons growing into serial killers.

Babies, on the other hand, were considered blank slates—tabula rasa—ready to be imprinted by whoever held them. Ursula was likely given this spiel in the unwed mothers home before she gave birth to me. Babies from unwed mothers "deserved a better home than their own mothers could provide" was the likely refrain of the nuns and caseworkers.

In the Domecon program it was documented that one practice mother put a baby down for a nap and another, different mother, was there when the baby awoke. Can you imagine the baby's confusion? How could a baby attach to anyone with so many arms holding him or her?

Ursula didn't get the chance to even be a practice mother, though she told me she'd tried. She'd asked to hold me, she said, before I was whisked away to the nursery, and then forever gone. The nurses let her, but they also said, "Don't get attached."

———

A crying baby doesn't know what is wrong; it just knows something is wrong. A baby is vulnerable, and so is its brain. It's the job of the parent, the mother many would say, to soothe their baby, to determine what is wrong and make it better. The emerging scientific field of epigenetics—the study of biological mechanisms that turn genes on and off—is clear that a close, intimate, and immediate bond with the mother lays the foundation for a calmer baby and a well-adjusted adult.

"Imagine if the hugs, lullabies and smiles from parents could inoculate babies against heartbreak, adolescent angst and even help them pass their exams decades later. Well, evidence from the new branch of science called epigenetics is reporting that this long-term emotional inoculation might be possible," researchers from the *London Journal of Primary Care* wrote in a report titled "The importance of early bonding on the long-term mental health and resilience of children."

These days, researchers studying maternal attachment recommend zero separation of mother and child. The best environment for a baby is skin-to-skin with its mother.

———

When my grandson was born, my eldest son and daughter-in-law praised the benefits of being skin-to-skin with him. They carved out time to be alone with him and made boundaries for how his first days and weeks would be so they could cuddle and hold him. I'd raised a son so committed to his baby that he knew the words *lanugo* (the soft hairs that cover a newborn's body) and *vernix* (the greasy, protective coating babies are born with). Maybe I'd broken the cycle of abandonment by raising my boys to be healthy and happy adults. Look what I've done, I thought. I felt overjoyed.

———

I think of all the babies, toddlers, and children separated from their mothers at the border. Some, it's been reported, have forgotten their mother's faces. Even if they are reunited, they may appear as changelings—fairy children left in place of human children.

———

Donald Aldinger, a Domecon practice baby who reconnected at forty-six with four of his practice mothers said, "For the first time in my life I feel like everybody else who had a family."

———

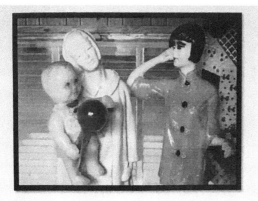

Image   RT-AB-13
Year   1949
Topic   Resident Teaching > Apartment Babies
Text   Charlie, November 1949, Norma Keagle, Barbara McCann.

One wonders what effect composite mothering has upon babies themselves. If a baby misses the love of the mother one must remember that all these babies are institution babies. Also the period of shifting care is brief and one in which the ideal feeding scheldule greatly outweighs the disadvantages.

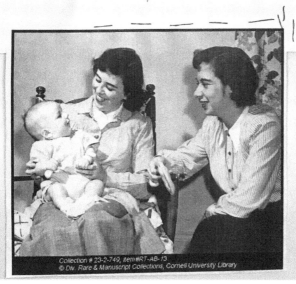

Composite Mothering.
Courtesy of Div. of Rare & Manuscript Collections, Cornell University.

———

I could call my playing with dolls an experiment but my years as a science writer taught me that experiments begin with a hypothesis—a question in search of an answer; a starting point for investigation. My play began innocently until I took a step back and began asking some hard questions of myself. Why this particular dollhouse? Why these dolls? Why did I love the babies so much? I'd collected six of them within the month.

I wasn't thinking about "making art" with these dolls. I was procrastinating writing and trying to keep my hands busy. There were three visual artists in residence with me and I talked with them about their work and loved to watch them create. Together, we took trips to the local thrift stores and Goodwill because we shared a passion for using found objects in our art. I used what I had on hand: white copier paper, a black and white printer, my dolls and dollhouse, and a travel sewing kit a previous resident had left in the drawer of the bedside table. I set about using needle and thread to stitch together the paper on which I'd printed the images. I strung up what resembled a clothesline with cotton twine from the junk drawer in the kitchen. I hung the photos with a handful of doll-sized clothespins that had garnished the fancy cocktails we drank downtown.

Any time I was vexed in my writing, I sewed another set of photographs together and hung it in my studio. I stepped back one day and realized it had the effect of a doll-sized clothesline. Without realizing it, I had mimicked some of the domestic tasks—sewing and laundry—that had been taught to the young women in Cornell's practice apartment.

When I mounted my show in an art gallery, visitors stood gaping at the photos. After reading my artist statement about the Domecon babies, I overheard them say, "That isn't real, is it? That can't be real."

————

I look on the Internet to see what sort of brace I might have worn to heal my hips. I find photos of baby dolls trussed up to demonstrate how to properly brace an infant's legs. There are two main types of braces for hip dysplasia: the soft Pavlik Harness, which positions the baby like a splayed chicken, or the hard Hip Abduction Bar, which looks like Tiny Tim stuck his cane horizontally between the knees. Both braces set the legs wide at the hip in a frog-like position reminiscent of Happy Baby pose in yoga.

In this contraption, I'd have been hard to hold. Besides, it was strictly advised that the braces remain in place except for bathing and diapering. Mom told me I'd had to continue sleeping in a brace for months after they'd adopted me.

The words used to describe what happened to my hip sockets—instability, prone to dislocation—could also have described my feelings as a child.

————

How else to express the term mother who isn't one's biological mother without saying "caregiver" or "nurse"? How else to identify a human child, someone's son or daughter, as an object: a thing to practice or play with, a doll?

Since I became aware of the Domecon babies, I've wanted to seek them out, talk to them, but most importantly I wanted to hold them.

Being held tight is what I desire most. Being held tight also terrifies me.

————

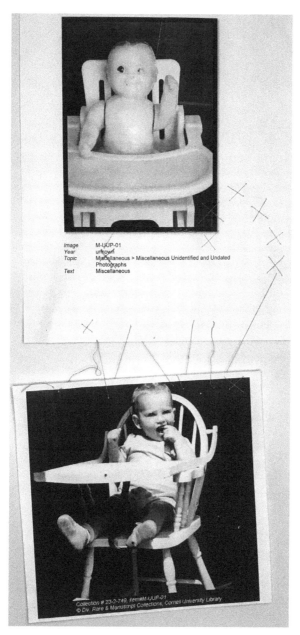

Image   M-UUP-01
Year   unknown
Topic   Miscellaneous > Miscellaneous Unidentified and Undated
        Photographs
Text   Miscellaneous

Unknown/Miscellaneous.
Courtesy of Div. of Rare & Manuscript Collections, Cornell University.

———

At the time the degree program in Domestic Economics was conceived, the scientific art of childrearing was broadly called "Mothercraft." These principles urged mothers not to cuddle their babies, as coddling was considered detrimental and could lead to the child being spoiled. This meant it was unacceptable to soothe a crying infant.

Let the child cry, the science of the times advised. Let the babe soothe itself.

Soothing my own crying sons made me feel I had motherly superpowers. I cooed to them, sang to them, rocked them, and let them fall asleep, skin-to-skin, on my chest.

It was when I couldn't soothe them that I'd become near hysterical, fearful of what was wrong that I couldn't appease. Why couldn't I make them stop crying? Surely I'd failed as a mother. When it came time for my eldest son to cry himself to sleep, I sat outside his door and bawled silently—knees to my chin in a tight ball—until I heard his heaving sobs taper into whimpers and then into the silence of snorts and sleep. After twenty minutes, I tiptoed into his room to gaze down at his tiny face and whisper apologies. "I'm sorry, I'm so sorry."

I later learned that this technique is called "Ferberizing," also known as "graduated extinction." Named after Richard Ferber, physician and the director of The Center for Pediatric Sleep Disorders at Children's Hospital Boston, it is an infant sleep-training program that aims to deny a child access to the parents in order to get them to soothe themselves by "crying it out." In his 1985 book, *Solve Your Child's Sleep Problems*, Ferber advocates letting a baby cry for up to forty-five minutes.

As a new mother, I never even thought to question the savagery of this technique.

———

"How do you self-soothe?" my therapist asked.

"I suppose I compartmentalize my feelings," I said.

I have a difficult time asking for help. I rarely cry, even while my body begs for the catharsis and relief of tears. I long to ugly-cry in someone's arms, yet I'm terrified that I might be inconsolable.

I've rationalized that my cries in that foster home didn't bring my foster mother running to comfort me. Over time I've learned to keep silent, to turn my suffering upon myself and to not trust anyone to appropriately comfort me. In keeping with the child-rearing science of the times—and considering my hip and leg braces—I was likely held only when I was fed or diapered. My decades-long bout with bulimia can no doubt be traced to seeking comfort in food I thought might never come, or that was given on a strict timeline as was likely the case in my infancy and similar to the experience of the Domecon babies.

I seek out hugs from others. I give warm, tight hugs. I was a hugger for the Special Olympics. I desire to be held so closely that I melt into the person holding me and yet I also have a fear of being let go. In that "letting go" is the implication that the person won't return, and with it comes a deep distrust that I will not be abandoned. The act of being held, therefore, translates into a fear of being left.

"What you fear is what you were deprived of," my therapist said.

"What do you think it is I fear?" I said.

"Maybe, that you will be unable to seek comfort," she said.

———

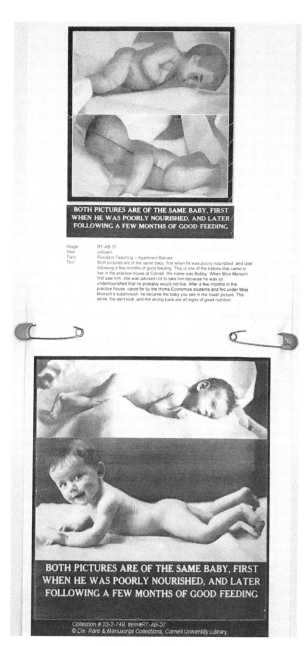

Sick baby/Well baby.
Courtesy of Div. of Rare & Manuscript Collections, Cornell University.

Courses in Cornell's Domestic Economy curriculum re-lied on making a science of everyday tasks such as home-making, budgeting, food preparation, and motherhood. But quantifying the act of childrearing by turning it into a science seemed oddly unnatural, and resulted in strict regimens for eating, sleeping, feeding, and bathing—like this sample daily schedule.

Sample Schedule for a Domestic Economy Baby (16–18 months)

7:00	Chair (urination)
7:30	Cereal with milk
8:30	Orange or prune juice, and cod liver oil
9:00	Chair (urination)
10:00	Bath
10:30	Chair (urination)
	Bottle then nap
1:15	Chair (urination)
1:30	Vegetable, bacon (occasionally), egg custard or egg milk, and Zwieback
2:00	Chair (bowel movement)
2–5:30	Playtime (may receive guests)
3–4:00	Wheeled out in carriage or taken for a walk
4:30	Vegetable soup or beef juice or broth
	Zwieback or graham crackers
6:30	Undress
	Cereal and bottle
	Chair (urination)
	Bed
10:00	Chair (urination)

The mimeographed schedule that was sent home with me contained notes from the placement coordinator for my soon-to-be parents. I know this because my mother saved it in my Adopted Child's Baby Book. My schedule was strict with feeding, bathing, and sleeping noted in hourly, sometimes 15-minute increments just as it was for the Domecon babies. It also contained brief notes such as:

COMMENTS: Baby seldom cries unless she is hungry or she has to burp. Baby sometimes skips a day to have a bowel movement but this does not bother her at all.

BABY LIKES: To be with people—dangling toys—to chew on something hard such as a bread stick—to hold her blanket in her hand when she takes a bottle or goes to sleep.

By contrast, the advice I was given for raising and feeding my sons consisted of phrases like "let them nurse when they're hungry," "forget the housework," and "sleep when the baby sleeps."

In archival photos, the Domecon practice apartment was appointed to mimic everyday life, yet it was void of the actual trappings of real life. There are images of co-eds vacuuming in front of near-empty bookshelves, and the nursery was outfitted with a one-way mirror where co-eds observed a practice mother caring for a baby from another room as if they were in a living laboratory. No one lived full-time in that practice house. They may have slept there for a night or two, but mostly the co-eds appeared between classes and perhaps to make meals, or to hand off a practice baby to another mother.

They took courses titled: Foods and Nutrition, Elementary Sewing, Handicraft and Cookery, Household Management & The Apartment Problem. There was a six-week "Charm School" that taught women cosmetics, fashion budgeting, and what to appropriately wear. There was the popular "Marriage Course," taught by Lemo Rockwood. Professor Rockwood described her course as the teaching, among other things, of "scientific information which has promoted the study of mate choice and marital adjustment; the development of affection in the individual, and the achievement of heterosexuality."

The curricular literature noted: "To most of the girls who have never been held responsible for a child, the job of mother is the most bewildering of any in the apartment."

All these teachings, to me, seemed to take the nurture right out of nature and were quite in keeping with the anti-nurture sentiment of the times. The practice baby program is so dystopian it is listed on the *Ripley's Believe it or Not!* website.

———

The antonym for *nurture* is *neglect*.

———

Mothercraft.
Courtesy of Div. of Rare & Manuscript
Collections, Cornell University.

I was not a violent child. In fact, I tried to be the perfect child.

Studies indicate there are two archetypes of the adopted child—one who pushes boundaries and seeks negative attention (making parents and siblings exhaustingly reinforce and demonstrate their bottomless love), and the perfectionist who tries to be the model child, who does not make waves, who rarely asks for help, and who never openly seeks attention and love. Both archetypes manifest a fear of abandonment in different ways.

My adoptive parents weren't big on hugging. They didn't withhold affection, per se, and looking back perhaps they were likely taking cues from me. My mom used to say I was "very independent" and could "play by myself for hours." I suppose being self-contained was my means of protection, some sort of invisibility cloak that allowed me to disappear inside my own head. I've been told I am "mysterious and complicated." I suppose this is another way of expressing my invisibility, or my unwillingness to be seen.

The real me is embodied in the fears I rarely voice. I am fearful of never truly being seen or loved for who I am. If I don't let myself be truly seen, however, was I ever really here? In other words, have I "othered" myself? Have I abandoned myself?

As if to reinforce her projection of my wholesomeness, Mom bought me a Holly Hobbie doll. "Start each day in a happy way," was Holly's tagline.

When I was sad as a child Mom used to say, "I just want everything to be perfect." She wanted our lives to be perfect, not in a negative way; in a good way. The trouble is that repeatedly hearing the phrase had the opposite effect on me. Those words came with an unintended impact that reinforced the notion that if I wasn't perfect, or didn't act perfectly, there would be consequences. Maybe, like the Domecon babies, I could be returned if my parents weren't satisfied. I see now with adult eyes that this is exactly the fear of abandonment my therapist described.

I wasn't perfect. I had dark thoughts. I did bad things. I didn't let my parents see those parts of me. Had they seen the heaps of vomit gathered outside my bedroom window? Had they noticed the scabs I picked at continuously that formed scars on my thighs? Had they read my diary of self-loathing? Did they know I sat, curled in the dark in my bedroom closet composing music? I titled my first piece *Persephone* before I understood the myth of how she was abducted by Hades to be his bride in the underworld; before I read how her mother, Demeter, moved heaven and earth to find her.

I defaced Holly Hobbie. I rimmed her eyes with black marker, making them heavy with inky eyeliner, and cut her dirty blond hair so short that it stuck out 90-degrees from her head and showed swaths of pink plastic scalp. I pierced her ears with Mom's quilting pins, stripped her naked, held her chubby plastic legs together by their flat feet and banged her head against the sharp edge of my desk. When her head wouldn't pop off, I ripped it off to see how it attached to her body.

Was I not a violent child?

Like me, Holly was flat chested and dressed in clothing straight out of the *Little House on the Prairie* TV series I loved to watch. Her plastic chest had no nipples, and the area where her vulva should have been was smooth between her thighs. Holly had an enormous out-of-scale head. Had she been rendered in flesh and blood the sheer weight of her skull would have snapped her dainty neck. She had only the hint of a nose, and no mouth whatsoever.

Had she wanted to speak her mind, she wouldn't have been able to do so.

———

In 1970, a psychologist named Mary Ainsworth identified three main attachment styles: secure, anxious, and avoidant. These attachment styles resulted from early interactions with the mother.

My therapist recommended I discover what my attachment style was in order to better understand how I relate to others, particularly men.

Like many adoptees, I found I was "anxiously attached," which means I crave closeness and intimacy, yet am insecure about how the other person feels about me—no matter how much they tell me otherwise. My near-constant fear of abandonment can send me into a spiral of internal neediness. My attachment style is attracted and attractive to men with "avoidant attachment" style—those who fear intimacy, or who are emotionally unavailable. As I write this now, I have been divorced for four years. In trying to date post-divorce I find I am a magnet for married and/or emotionally unavailable men. In other words, I am attracted and attractive to the very kind of man I fear most: one who will likely abandon me. Until I break the cycle, I will continue to play out my fear by seeking out and attracting men who will keep me in this demented comfort zone that replicates the hardwired experience of my abandonment as a baby.

————

In his 1959 experiment "Love in Infant Monkeys," Harry F. Harlow tested mother-child attachment bonds by isolating infant monkeys for up to thirty days in cages. He then created surrogate "mother" monkeys, one of bare wire and the other of wire covered with terry cloth to which the infants could cling. The infants who clung to the terry-cloth surrogate "mother" suffered less stress when they were brought out of isolation and were able to self-soothe.

"Suffering less" is still suffering.

The infant monkeys with the bare wire-framed mother figure had nothing to cling to.

Emerging from their isolation, they threw themselves on the floor clutching their heads, screaming, and crying. Two babies starved themselves to death.

Harlow also placed his baby monkey subjects in total isolation for the first eight months of life, denying them contact with other infants or with either type of surrogate mother. They emerged with permanent damage.

In the 1970s Harlow developed what was called "The Pit of Despair" to reproduce an animal model of clinical depression. He took baby and infant monkeys away from their mothers and isolated them in small wire cages. The monkeys soon became extremely depressed, stopped playing and interacting—some stopped eating.

These experiments were unethical, but Harlow's work did legitimize parenthood, adopted or otherwise, over institutionalized childcare. His experiments both normalized and pathologized adoption.

———

There is a long history of using orphans and children in psychological experiments. In 1945, Austrian-American psychologist René Árpád Spitz studied children in orphanages and foundling hospitals in South America. Spitz followed two groups of children from infancy until they were a few years old. One group was raised in an orphanage, and another group in a prison nursery with incarcerated mothers.

In the orphanage the babies were cut off from human contact and lay isolated in their cribs. A single nurse cared for seven children. The incarcerated mothers gave their babies care and affection every day. Additionally, the babies could see each other and the prison staff throughout the day.

At a year old, the two groups differed immensely. The babies raised in orphanages lagged far behind those reared in the prison nursery on every level. They were less curious, less playful, and didn't have the same motor or intellectual skills. Of the nearly thirty orphans, only two were walking, and those two could only manage a few words.

Spitz coined the term "anaclitic depression"—partial emotional deprivation as a result of the loss of a loved object (in this case the mother.) His findings showed that a lack of love and comfort could, in fact, have grave consequences on children. Babies who were not held can be stunted emotionally and physically. Some research has shown that if the situation persists, it can be deadly. The 1947 documentary *Grief: A Peril in Infancy* captured Spitz' findings. I don't recommend watching it.

Psychologist John Bowlby along with Spitz conducted what would be the first studies into the theory that evolved into what the DSM now calls "attachment disorder."

A 1998 article in the *New York Times Magazine* detailed attachment theory as the ultimate experiment.

"Bowlby's early research had been with children who had undergone traumatic separations from their parents—children in foundling homes and child-guidance clinics, young evacuees from the London blitz and otherwise happy children confined to the hospital in an era when visiting hours, even for mothers and fathers, were normally restricted to once a week," wrote reporter Margaret Talbot. "In all of these cases, Bowlby detected an initial stage of protest, followed by a kind of passive grief or dejection that could sometimes appear to be cooperative behavior to busy nurses or social workers, followed by a deeper and lasting emotional detachment—the child might be cheerful with others, but defensively reject his mother when she appeared again."

Victor Groza is a contemporary researcher and adoption specialist at Case Western Reserve University who has conducted several studies on the emotional and behavioral development of Romanian adoptees.

"The children adopted from Romanian institutions represent an opportunity to examine the effects of deprivation on child development comparable to experimental research conducted on primates," Groza said.

"Continuity of affectionate care by one or a small number of caregivers who can give of themselves emotionally, as well as in other ways, originates the development of the child's love relationships," wrote Linda Mayes and Sally Provence, both professors of child development at Yale University. "Having repeated experiences of being comforted when distressed, for instance, is a part of developing one's own capacity for self-comfort and self-regulation, and later, the capacity to provide the same for others."

———

In 1952, psychoanalyst Donald Woods (D. W.) Winnicott, whose work helped inform attachment theory, coined the term "comfort object." The object could be a doll, teddy bear, or blanket which—together with what Winnicott called a "good enough mother"—helps a child learn to slowly transition and separate from its mother.

"It is true that the piece of blanket (or whatever it is) is symbolical of some part-object, such as the breast," wrote Winnicott in his 1953 paper, "Transitional Objects and Transitional Phenomena—A Study of the First Not-Me Possession," in *The International Journal of Psychoanalysis.* "Nevertheless the point of it is not its symbolic value so much as its actuality. Its not being the breast (or the mother) although real is as important as the fact that it stands for the breast (or mother).

"When symbolism is employed the infant is already clearly distinguishing between fantasy and fact, between inner objects and external objects, between primary creativity and perception. But the term transitional object, according to my suggestion, gives room for the process of becoming able to accept difference and similarity. I think there is use for a term for the root of symbolism in time, a term that describes the infant's journey from the purely subjective to objectivity; and it seems to me that the transitional object (piece of blanket, etc.) is what we see of this journey of progress towards experiencing."

———

When I am anxious I sleep with my Bun-Bun, a yellow stuffed rabbit given to me by my grandmother when I was about two years old. He is bare in places where I've rubbed off his fur. (I called this "fuzzying" when I was a child.) I've had to re-embroider his pink nose and black mouth.

––––––

Experiments like these show the negative effects of separating children from mothers and parents, and the effects on a child's secure development to themselves and on future relationships. Many would argue these scientific experiments reinforced what is already known of human development—a baby will better develop if it remains with its mother. The idea that scientific methods needed to overlay or short-circuit the instincts of mother and baby is indeed ludicrous, but perhaps only with hindsight. That this research was used to bludgeon mothers to stay in the home and to demonize them for leaving their children (in the care of others for instance) in order to enter the workplace, further underscores the demonization of women and the paradox of motherhood in all forms.

I suppose the founders of the Domecon program didn't set out to do harm, but the unintended negative consequence to those babies seems a non-starter.

––––––

Unfortunately babies and young children
make perfect scapegoats since they manifest
so nakedly all the sins that flesh is heir to:

they are selfish, jealous, sexy, dirty, and
given to tempers, obstinacy, and greed.
—John Bowlby, *The Making and
Breaking of Affectional Bonds*

———

Image   RT-AB-49
Year   unknown
Topic   Resident Teaching > Apartment Babies
Text   A student "mother-of-that-week" living in one of the homemaking apartments prepares the days formula for the "practice" baby for whom she is responsible.

While mothers are constantly changing the care remains constant and unvarying.

Mother of that week.
Courtesy of Div. of Rare & Manuscript Collections, Cornell University.

———

Martha Van Rensselaer and Flora Rose were co-founders of Cornell's Domestic Economics program, the first full female professors at the college, and advocates for suffrage and women's rights. They were also lovers who lived together for twenty-four years. They were so feared and revered that they were collectively referred to as 'Miss Van Rose.'

Van Rensslear's vision engaged the leading feminists of the time: Eleanor Roosevelt, Ida Tarbell, and Susan B. Anthony. The First Lady paid a campus visit to Van Rensselaer to advocate for an expansion of the concepts of home to include community, the nation, and the world. Van Rensselaer was recognized by The League of Women Voters as one of the twelve most important women in America.

If I step back and look at the Domecon experiment in motherhood and child rearing, it boils down to women observing women. Young ladies in the practice apartments were under close observation by their teachers, by each other, by science, and by society. The kitchen looked like a laboratory with beakers and scientific-like instruments. There was an observation room with a one-way mirror into the nursery where students and teachers monitored practice babies and practice mothers. I think about them all living in the human equivalent of a dollhouse. Theirs was a fake home set up with fake tasks and a fake baby: everyone playing at a life.

At the same time "Miss Van Rose" were preparing young women as "apprentice mothers," they were also keeping babies from—and in some cases taking them away from—their birth mothers.

———

Dicky Domecon, the first of all the practice babies at Cornell, was born on March 25, 1920, to a woman named Mae LaRock. He weighed 9 lb. 3 oz. and she named him Richard after Dr. Richards who helped with the birth. According to records, the birth father left Mae long before his son was born and, whether she realized it or not, Mae signed away the legal rights to her son before she left the hospital. Nowhere can I find how old Mae was when she gave birth.

By all accounts, Richard LaRock was a healthy baby. I imagine Martha Van Rensselaer happily picking him out of an infant lineup at one of the many orphanages or asylum homes with which she had agreements. He was plump and happy-looking with big, round eyes like a chubby doll.

He was renamed Dicky Domecon and placed immediately into the care of his practice mothers in the practice apartment at Cornell. His six or so mothers "fell in love with him."

Identity is a shifty thing with orphans and adoptees: perhaps even more so with the practice babies. Dicky was likely thought of as a tabula rasa. Imagine the trauma for an infant who had six mothers? He may not have known whom to focus on since the moment he got comfortable with one "mother," a shift change brought him a different face. He would have gone to sleep at night in the arms of one woman and awakened to the gaze of another. Even the spelling of Dicky's name was careless: I found him referred to as Dicky, Dickey, and Dickie.

On August 24, 1920, just as the co-eds were readying to return to campus, Flora Rose received a pleading letter from Dicky's mother, Mae, who was living less than two hours away in Oswego, New York.

"May I please come to see him?" wrote Mae of her son. "I love him and am very lonesome for him. If not, will you please write to me about him? Believe me I would be very grateful."

Flora Rose passed the letter along to Mrs. Florence Grannis, Commissioner for Placing Dependent Children, and wrote she "felt sorry for the mother and hoped she would have the chance to raise Dicky herself."

As the end of the term drew near, almost one year and a couple days to the date of Dicky's birth, March 24, 1921, Flora Rose wrote, "The question of letting Dickey go has been a very burning one with us, for we have grown to love the little boy and are deeply interested in him." On March 28, Rose wrote she would like to see Dickey placed with his biological mother. Commissioner Grannis, however, was convinced a good adoptive home would be found, because "everyone wants the child that is so desirable after the care he received at Cornell."

There is no further correspondence that indicates where Dickey was placed, if Mae was contacted, or if mother and son ever saw each other again.

————

When my sons were born I didn't want to let them go. In the surgical room, shivering from the C-sections under a light blanket, I clocked their trajectory from my eviscerated uterus to the weigh station. I demanded the nurses wheel them into my sight line and demanded they unstrap my arms so I could hold them immediately. I was terrified when they went out of my sight at night in the hospital nursery, or off to get circumcised. Where did this terror come from? Was it that I felt I'd been reborn in my sons? Did I innately fear they'd be whisked away as I was from my birth mother with the nurse warning, "Don't get attached"?

I took every opportunity to hold my boys until they wouldn't let me. I read to them every night, their heads cradled under the crook of my arm. I kissed them and let them sit on my lap to cuddle. I let them fall asleep on my chest and spooned them in their toddler beds when they were sick. Their fears were my fears and I did my best to soothe them and let them know I'd always be there for them: that I loved them unconditionally and that I'd never leave.

———

The behaviorist John Broadus Watson and his graduate student Rosalie Rayner conducted the Little Albert experiments in 1920. Watson was president of the American Psychological Association, a leading thinker at the time, and programs like Cornell's were based on the principles his science espoused: molding human behavior by scientific control.

His findings on child rearing included: firm feeding, sleeping, and toileting schedules (no matter if the child was hungry or sleepy). Pacifiers, thumb sucking, and any form of affection were strictly forbidden.

"When you are tempted to pet your child remember that mother love is a dangerous instrument," said Watson. "Never hug or kiss (your children), never let them sit on your lap."

Within the decade, Watson's experiments were deemed unethical and he was thrown out of the American Psychological Association. He and Rayner's extra-marital affair led to a spectacular end to his marriage and an academic ethics controversy.

But the vestiges of his ideas lingered for decades. Many psychologists believed that showing affection toward your child would spread disease and lead to problems in adulthood.

The Little Albert Experiment seemed an extension of the Pavlovian classical conditioning experiments with dogs. It made me wonder about my own abandonment issues. Was I scared of others abandoning me because I'd been classically conditioned to fear it? Did the fact that I wasn't comforted when I cried make me fearful of intimacy altogether?

Of the practice of using practice babies, a 1954 article in *Time Magazine* quoted Mrs. Babette Penner, director of the Women's Services Division of United Charities saying, "Imagine what anxieties there are in a child who is given a bottle in twelve or more pairs of arms."

———

In searching for a way to heal what felt like the broken child inside me, I decided I wanted to volunteer in a hospital maternity ward to hold babies. I thought I'd be giving them what they needed—closeness and attachment—but really it was what I desperately needed. I needed to be held like a baby.

Turns out it's impossible to get near a maternity ward these days. Back in the 1900s it seemed they were giving infants away. Today, I was politely redirected that I could volunteer in the gift shop, or the thrift shop, or at the visitor information desk. In short, there was no fucking way I was getting near any babies.

I read in the Domecon archives that one of the program's administrators said, "You have to remember, these are institution babies"—as if they were disposable, living dolls; objects to dress up, feed, and play with—pretty accessories for the girls to prance around with to show men how marriageable and motherly they were.

Studies of babies who have been orphaned or institutionalized have described them as exhibiting stereotyped movements like mirroring their caregiver, using self-stimulation, and having an empty look in their eyes.

"They cried vaguely or softly many times a day and seemed unhappy. Many of these children seemed depressed and unresponsive to initiatives for interaction, as if resigned to affective deprivation."

As an adult, I remember seeing the first-ever photo of myself as a four-month-old. It was given to me by my Catholic Charities caseworker. I recognized the vacant look in my infant eyes, same as the one described in all this research. Maybe I'd been classically conditioned, like Little Albert, to fear something. I had the vague notion that what I feared most was crying, both because once I started, I'd be unable to stop, but more so that no one would come to soothe me.

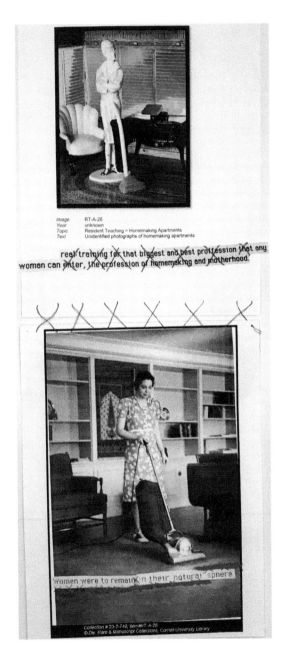

Image   RT-A-26
Year   unknown
Topic   Resident Teaching > Homemaking Apartments
Text   Unidentified photographs of homemaking apartments

real training for that biggest and best proffession that any
woman can enter, the profession of homemaking and motherhood.

Women were to remain in their natural sphere

Collection # 23-2-749, Item #RT-A-26
© Div. Rare & Manuscript Collections, Cornell University Library

Their "natural sphere."
Courtesy of Div. of Rare & Manuscript Collections, Cornell University.

———

My adopted mother, in offering me advice about my two sons, told me to put them in the playpen because of how well I'd fared there. "You loved to play by yourself in your playpen," she said. "You'd sit there for hours playing with your little plastic beads."

My attempts to cage my boys, who were slightly feral, curious, and strong, failed miserably. Once, when I put them both in the playpen outside so I could hang the laundry on the line, they crawled to one side together, pulled themselves up to stand, and shoved their little bodies against the sides to upend the entire playpen before crawling out.

———

In nineteenth-century New York, hospitals, homes, and almshouses began the practice of building "baby baskets" or "boxes" inside exterior doors into which a parent (usually an unwed mother) could place her infant. "Foundling wheels" have been around since medieval times, when Pope Innocent III had them built in churches so women could leave unwanted children instead of drowning them in the Tiber. In late-1800s New York, women held the title of "baby finder" or "baby farmer." Their job was to roam the city seeking out babies abandoned in public parks and on the streets. But many babies weren't, in fact, abandoned.

Baby farmers also collected infants of those single mothers who were working as domestic servants and wet nurses, breastfeeding the children of wealthy mothers, in homes of other wealthy mother's children. Their own babies were unwelcome in those homes.

"If these working mothers were unable to keep up with the payments for their children's board, baby farmers sent them to the almshouse where they were placed with homeless women living there who may or may not have been able to breastfeed," wrote Julie Miller in her book *Abandoned: Foundlings in 19th Century New York*. "Most [babies] raised in the almshouse did not survive."

Babies were abandoned in fields, on streets, and in parks. The practice was so prevalent that organizations taking in such infants began to name them by the streets, parks, and fields in which they were found. They were given names like James Secondstreet (1821) and William Bleecker (1838). Little Elizabeth Houston (1841) was found on the corner of Elizabeth and Houston; James Bowery (1860) in the Bowery, and Jane Broadway (1863) on Broadway. Babies found in City Hall Park were given the last name Park; others took on the last name Alley for having been found abandoned in an alley.

Babies were also given names of fictional and real-life orphans—Oliver Twist, Phineas T. Barnum, or worse, by the simple fact they'd been abandoned: Henry Foundling, or William Unknown.

———

Since 1999, when it was first enacted in Texas, each US state now has what's called a Safe Haven Law, which allows parents to relinquish infants in a safe place, such as a hospital, firehouse, or police station. The laws were intended to prevent what have been called "Dumpster Babies," newborns abandoned in dumpsters by frightened people, usually women. The idea is that an infant won't come to harm and the parent won't suffer negative consequences.

In 2008, Nebraska expanded the law to include children up to nineteen years of age. One father, Gary Staton, abandoned nine of his ten children who ranged in age from one to seventeen years. "He could no longer cope with the burden of raising them," the article said.

His wife had died giving birth to their tenth child.

———

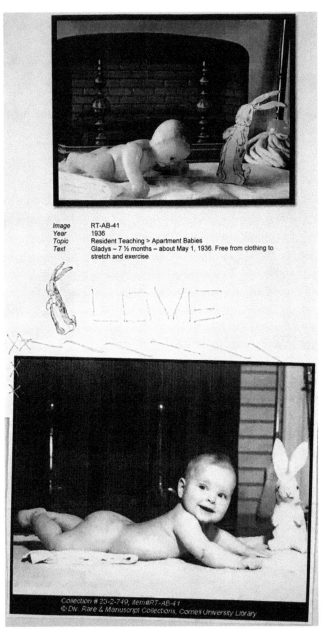

Image	RT-AB-41
Year	1936
Topic	Resident Teaching > Apartment Babies
Text	Gladys – 7 ½ months – about May 1, 1936. Free from clothing to stretch and exercise.

Gladys Free from Clothing.
Courtesy of Div. of Rare & Manuscript Collections, Cornell University.

———

When I began the search for my birth mother, I had little information. I had a doctored birth certificate, the Internet was barely functional, and the path to "finding" seemed a messy one fraught with complications. As an adoptee, I had to willingly open myself up to the idea of being abandoned again.

Abandonment seems a harsh word. Having met my birth mother, I have no doubt she viewed giving me up as surrender. Surrendering a baby is, in itself, a form of surrender. I have no doubt she thought she was doing the right thing.

My birth name was Gabriella Herman. My adoptive name is Megan Gabriella Culhane. Like the Domecon Babies I was in a "home" that wasn't my home, with a "mother" who wasn't my mother. My identity was erased once, and in order to possess my original birth certificate, I'd have to obtain a valid ID that showed who I was before I became who I am. My birth mother and I could literally walk into the Office of Vital Records in NYC, vouch for each other as kin, and I'd still be denied access to my original birth certificate.

———

Eventually, the law in New York changed to give adoptees access to their original birth records. Children born in New York, as I was, can now request their "Pre-Adoption Birth Certificate." I filled out the forms and mailed in my $45 check to the Office of Vital Records just as the COVID-19 pandemic hit. I'm still waiting to receive my original birth certificate.

"Where you came from informs who you are, and every New Yorker deserves access to the same birth records—it's a basic human right," Governor Andrew Cuomo said. "For too many years, adoptees have been wrongly denied access to this information."

———

I was holding my grandson when he was about five months old. We were in the rocking chair at my son's house and I held him until he fell asleep: his tiny mouth breathing hot on my neck and drooling. I hummed the chorus of Suzanne Vega's "Gypsy" while I rocked him. *Oh, hold me like a baby.* It occurred to me then that he was the same age I'd been when my parents adopted me. I kissed the top of his head. I held him tighter.

I'd been looking through my Adopted Child's Baby Book and found a photo of me at that same age. I compared my photo and his. I felt like I was looking at myself. I live for his smile now.

The bedroom we brought you home to

Happy Together

My parents hadn't expected the call so soon, so they only had two boxes of Pampers and a bureau Dad had antiqued blue. That night, they went shopping with Mom Mops, Pop Pops, and Aunt Muffin. They didn't know where to begin. "We all ran around buying anything we saw for babies," Mom wrote in the section titled "What We Thought When We Heard the News" in my Adopted Child's Memory Book.

The next day they went to the appointment and Mrs. Legare, the adoption coordinator at Catholic Charities, told them all about me. They couldn't wait to see me on Thursday. They spent the next two days shopping and trying to visualize what I'd look like. They spent a frantic day moving Dad's den furniture from my room to the front room.

"We were in turmoil," wrote my mother.

———

My father, Michael, was an English teacher at Rippowam High School in Stamford, Connecticut. He'd been in seminary, destined for the priesthood, until he saw my mother riding in a Chevy II convertible in a parade through downtown Norwalk. She was the head baton twirler for the Norwalk High School marching band. I imagine her perched on the trunk with her feet resting on the back seat cradling the rubber of her baton in a fist at her hip; its silvery stem resting in the crook of her delicate elbow. Dad left the seminary. Pop Pop told me Dad's name meant "Son of God."

Mom's name was Roberta. She was the eldest daughter of a Depression-era Polish immigrant who owned a local body shop. Grampy owned two square blocks of prime Main Street real estate in South Norwalk. His tenants included welfare renters, the Owl restaurant, a Goodwill store, and a dubious bar called Diamond Jim's, which I'd always taken to be a strip club.

Mom twirled the baton in the marching band at UConn. She was a straight-A horticulture major and Dad's angel.

My parents made $5,000 a year in 1966. Their doctor had perhaps advised them that they would not be able to conceive. They had given up trying to have a child of their own and decided to adopt.

———

Thursday arrived and, after my father finished teaching his classes, they hurried over to Catholic Charities in Bridgeport, Connecticut, to meet me. They waited nervously until the receptionist told them to go downstairs. They walked down the stairs and started around the corner, and suddenly, there I was: chubby, with eyes as big as blue saucers and a crooked smile that (according to my mother) beguiled everyone. I was their baby. Mom said I didn't cry; I played with my toys; I ate what was in front of me, and posed for any and all pictures.

I was ruthlessly loved.

The year they brought me home, The Turtles sang "Happy Together," and kids danced to the Bug-a-Loo. I was nearly six months old, seventeen pounds, fifteen ounces, with my first two bottom teeth "just showing."

I came with the name Gabriella. My parents liked it so much they kept it as my middle name.

In my Adopted Child's Memory Book, my mother wrote of the day we met: "Mrs. Legare was holding you, and you had a big smile on your face. You were the opposite of what we had visualized. We expected a little skinny baby, and there you were—big and beautiful! Daddy held you on his lap, and you looked up at him and over at Mommy with your big blue eyes and never made a sound. After a bit of difficulty, your inexperienced Mom managed to get you into your pink corduroy snowsuit."

Angel, Archangel, Son of God: We formed a Trinity.

My parents took me home.

The bedroom we brought you home to.
Courtesy of Michael B. Culhane.

Your first birthday cake

An Adopted Child's
Memory Book

*Meeting My Birth Mother
for the First Time*

What I brought to meet you

My Medela breast pump, batteries and extra baby bottles; Virginia Slim menthol cigarettes; a pack of Trident peppermint gum; breath mints; $100 in cash; my Adopted Child's Memory Book; my favorite threadbare flannel pajamas; some of the columns I'd written in college; pictures of me as a child.

What I wore to meet you

Faded, soft, carpenter jeans with the hammer loop barely attached on the right side; black Doc-Marten wing-tips; a vintage pajama shirt from ZuZu's consignment store in Ithaca, NY, where they sold clothes by the pound; a Johnson Woolen Mills red and black checked hunting jacket that was my husband's grandfather's—the lining was missing and the left cuff was held together by a twig.

What you wore to meet me

A bright orange cashmere tunic sweater; earrings that dangled like Alexander Calder mobiles; pink lipstick that left a tiny spot on your right front tooth; bare feet with your nails polished red; eyeglasses that were striped lime green; a modern take on the cat eye. You changed frames many times that weekend to match your outfits. You called glasses, "jewelry for your face."

How I felt when I first saw you

Like the negative space in an Edgar Rubin image.

What I said when I first met you

"Hi, I'm your daughter."

What you said when you first met me

"I thought the front desk would call before letting you come up!"

What you looked like to me

I didn't recognize any similarities and thought, "maybe I have the wrong room." Then you hugged me.

My first pair of shoes

We were window-shopping and walked into The Gap on Lexington Avenue. I found a pair of shoes I liked, and at the register, you said, "These will be my treat." I protested that I had a fine enough job to pay for Gap shoes. As we walked out of the store, I laughed, "You just bought me my first pair of baby shoes . . . size 9 ½."

Stories you told me

Different versions of who my father was: Dick Sanford, whom you adored at the time and were dating steadily, or some other guy you'd slept with after Dick had left for the Navy. You said you were "90 percent sure" that Dick was my father, "although it pretty much could have been anyone, it was the late '60s."

What we cried about

"When you were a year old I convinced myself that I'd found where you lived," you said. "There was a girl I'd seen playing in the yard, and she was the age you would have been with brown hair and features I'd attributed to you in my mind. I convinced myself it was you. I needed to know you were all right. I hid in the bushes and watched you play. You were happy and healthy and had what seemed to be a good family. It made me feel better even though, deep down, I knew it wasn't you."

Stories I told you

That it was okay when you said you didn't know who exactly my father was; that the most important thing was that we had finally met; that now that you were in my life I felt the circle was complete.

Your first birthday cake.
Courtesy of Michael B. Culhane.

Muffin Lane: The house we brought you home to.

Consider the Lilies

Consider the lilies of the field, how they
grow; they toil not, neither do they spin.
—Matthew 6:28

Their bedroom: I knew it by heart. The Trojan condoms in the bottom drawer of Dad's nightstand; a copy of *The Bell Jar* on Mom's side; the shotgun in the back of the closet behind Oxford shoes; the corduroy sports jackets Dad wore to teach English at our high school.

Mom's dresser was a trove of white C-cup bras, half-slips, and a jewelry box that opened to a twirling ballerina in a white tutu. She had two kinds of perfume that sat atop her dresser: Shalimar by Guerlain and Cotillion by Avon. Shalimar smelled spicy and exotic, while Cotillion was powdery and delicate. They seemed to belong to two different women. Two women I wanted to be but didn't yet know how to become.

As a kid, I took tiny inventories of Mom's things, especially the jewelry in that box: the mother-of-pearl pin I gave her that said "Mother"; a lacquered red rose stick pin; a string of pearls she wore in her wedding portrait that hung in the hallway; the clothes on the hangers; the sensible shoes she kept in orderly boxes at the bottom of her closet; the Ginny dolls in polka dot boxes on the shelf whose eyes opened and closed and whose tiny leather shoes had silver snaps.

I conducted my inventories in secret, knowing Mom would feel it was an invasion of her privacy. I did it, perhaps, to hew to some form of identity for myself. I was adopted, and while it didn't occur to me consciously at that time, looking back, I realized I felt out of place. Or, maybe I was trying to find my place within the family via objects. Something always seemed to be missing for me, a piece of myself that I couldn't classify, something within me but at the same time unreachable. I couldn't put my finger on exactly what it was. I am not sure I will ever be able to recognize it.

––––––––

Next to Mom's dresser hung a framed print with a version of the then ubiquitous poem "Children Learn What They Live," by Dorothy Law Nolte.

*If children live with criticism, they learn to
   condemn . . .
If children live with shame, they learn to feel
   guilty . . .*

As a child, snooping about, I read the poem many times. It registered to me then as being powerful and more significant, but I didn't know what "apprehensive" meant or how to feel "envy" or how to connect all the similes within the poem. I didn't know what to feel because I realize now, I didn't know how to feel much of anything then. I was both inside my head and outside of myself. I took everything in and let nothing out. I gauged other people's reactions to my actions and then fine-tuned myself accordingly. I tried on personas like pants (one summer I announced to my cousins that I was going to be "preppy" in the upcoming year of junior high). I was trying to mold an identity based on how I was reflected in other people. I sought out external, positive validation, and when I got it (rarely), I questioned its validity.

Dad wanted me to be an Irish step dancer and a concert violinist. I balked at the former (the costumes! the fake hair!) but begged to play the violin starting in fourth grade. I had modest success: All-State orchestra and a small music scholarship to Penn State. I also absorbed Dad's disappointment that I didn't go to Juilliard, where my Juilliard-trained teacher at the time told me I could have gone.

Mom kept saying, "Be yourself." But with no explanation of what "self" I was supposed to be, I felt I was botching the whole thing. I was continually fighting with the image I saw in the mirror because I felt I was playing to an unsatisfied audience who seemed to be demanding their ticket money back.

I was a curious child. I poked around in Mom's things, messed through the drawers in her bathroom vanity, opened the tubes of Vagisil, took her Tampax out of the cardboard packaging and dropped them headfirst into the toilet water to watch them bloom like white lilies.

"Those aren't toys, they're expensive," she said, yet never explained to me what Tampax were used for.

When I finally got my period, at sixteen, during J.V. cheerleading practice, my friend Wendy passed me a Playtex tampon under the bathroom stall door. It was wrapped in pink plastic. She gave no explanation for how to use it, and I was too embarrassed to ask. I inserted it farther than I felt was comfortable, which was half as far as it needed to go. It hurt like hell. I spent the rest of cheerleading practice performing splits and jumps with that tampon neither inside of me nor out.

When I was in grammar school, I watched Mom get ready for cast parties. Dad was the theater director as part of his duties as an English teacher at our high school, and she was the one presented with bouquets of flowers before each production. She went to the cast parties with Dad after each play wrapped up the season. There were parties for *Flowers for Algernon*, *I Never Saw Another Butterfly*, *Bye Bye Birdie*, and *The Screwtape Letters* (which we were not allowed to see).

I spent much of my after-school time in middle school with Dad in the theater. I'd race up and down the carpeted stairs; unfold the theater seats and sit in every one as fast as I could; pose in ways that might attract the attention of all the high school leading men on whom I had consecutive crushes. Then I'd climb the stairs to the control booth and flirt with the boy operating the lights and the soundboard. At home, I cared for a white mouse that was a prop in *Flowers for Algernon*. I was a demented Eloise, and the high school theater was my Plaza Hotel.

It seems to me now that I was fusing myself onto other people, flailing around for someone I could identify with, trying to imitate, act, perform, or pretend my way into a character whose part wasn't scripted yet. I had no idea who I was.

Watching Mom get ready to go to the plays and the cast parties with Dad was magical because she seemed happy. She was so pretty, bobby-pinning her short brown hair into spit curls in front of her ears and pressing her lips on white Kleenex, leaving red puckered lipstick stains. I buzzed around her like a gnat, asking questions and bouncing on her bed. Eventually, Dad pulled into the driveway with our babysitter Kevin Silk and I skipped down the hall to fuss over him in all of his teenage cuteness.

The last thing Mom did before leaving the house was spray Cotillion on her wrists and behind her ears. Then she leaned over to kiss me goodnight on the top of my head. After she left I locked myself in her bathroom, picked the Kleenex out of the trash and squeezed my lips together where hers had been.

Shalimar was the expensive perfume Dad bought for Mom every single Christmas, along with a crisp white blouse with a lace collar. When we got older, Dad gave us girls money and instructions shortly before Christmas to "go pick out" these items for her. He made a big deal of it when she unwrapped the blouse or the perfume. I remember her face being flat and expressionless as she replaced the tissue paper and put the box with the blouse on the floor next to her chair before motioning us to open our gifts, which she had handmade. She was a furious knitter and an expert quilter and sewer. How did Dad expect her to be surprised by these same gifts given to her year after year? I think now that her expression was one of muted pain for living with a man who didn't understand her enough to know that Cotillion was the perfume she preferred.

Mom was practical and a master of the needle arts. She handled all the bill paying and the books. She balanced our checkbooks throughout college. She made lists, did the laundry, made dinner, and waited for Dad to come home. She enjoyed sewing her own clothes, and ours until we made a forceful stink about it. Her Singer sewing machine, a 16th birthday present from her mother, whirred as we crammed into our small TV room to watch *Mutual of Omaha's Wild Kingdom* and *Little House on the Prairie*. Dad put his feet up on the ottoman of his

Naugahyde easy chair and, post-shower, I sat on the floor with my legs outstretched and the plastic hair dryer cap billowing its soft heat onto my head. Mom sat in a straight-backed chair at her sewing machine and worked stitches into a piece of calico for one of her dresses. Every line of new stitches she sewed sent static fuzzing across our console TV.

"This makes me happy," I remember her saying, "all of us here together."

I watched that expensive perfume evaporate over the years. The Shalimar bottle, with its sapphire stopper and tiny gold tassel, sat next to Mom's jewelry box on her dresser. The white blouses moldered in her closet, collecting dust on their shoulders where they hung on plastic hangers. She would wear some of them when she went to work as a bank teller, pairing them with hand-sewn cotton skirts or jumpers. But mostly, like the Shalimar, the blouses were too fancy and frilly for her sensibility.

———

The same poem in the same frame now hangs above a dresser in my bedroom. It carries a heavier weight for me. If Mom were alive still, I might ask her what the poem meant to her. I might ask her if she felt, as I do, that parenting is as much a balancing act as a burden. I might ask her if she felt it was as hard as I do to take care of yourself when you are trying to launch your children into the world.

———

Mom wasn't much for expressing her feelings when she was alive. What she did express, most times, was exasperation. Exhaustion and obligation also shimmered off her like heat rising from beach sand.

I was in the backseat of the GM Sportabout. Mom had picked me up from middle school. It was sometime in the late seventies. We were on our way to my ballet lessons at the War Memorial. I was trying to use the backseat as a changing room, stripping off my school clothes and writhing into my pink dance tights and black leotard. Then as now, I was shy and anxious about my body. I tried lying down to take off my jeans and underwear to wiggle into my ballet tights, but that didn't work, so I tried crouching on the floor between the front and back seats. I tried to fashion a makeshift curtain with my coat to guard myself. As I slid my arm out of my shirt and into my leotard, I worked hard not to expose my undeveloped chest or my stomach that flabbed over the waistband of my jeans.

I remember Mom glancing in the rear-view mirror. Her exasperation seemed to me to heighten with every glance.

"Oh for God's sake, Megan, no one is looking at you."

But Mom was looking at me. She was watching me as much as I was watching her. I wonder who she thought she was looking at and why I seemed to exasperate her so much.

If a child lives with exasperation, (s)he learns to be invisible.

Our car rides were usually attended to in silence: Me trying to think of things to talk about with her, but being unsure of what to say or what she was thinking, and worrying that she was thinking about how disappointed she was with me. She was absorbed in her thoughts and driving me to and fro, it seemed, out of obligation. She was not about to let me in. So I let her be.

Eventually, when I was in sixth or seventh grade, Dad quit his teaching job to start his own contracting business and Mom had to go back to work. I couldn't get to my dance lessons anymore. She had been my ride. My ballet teacher, Mrs. Watley, called our house at dinner one night to see if I would be returning to class. I began to explain the situation, but I got choked up. I loved ballet.

"Oh, Megan, give it to me," Mom said, grabbing the mustard-colored phone receiver out of my hand. I sat back down at the dinner table and wondered what I'd done wrong. In hindsight, I think Mom was embarrassed perhaps thinking about my ballet teacher silently judging her to be a bad mother, but at the time I felt like I had done something to embarrass her. She may have been exasperated that she had to take that job at the bank. She hated that job, but did it to pay bills and afford us health insurance. Among other things, Dad had been diagnosed with diabetes. Maybe this is adult me overthinking twelve-year-old me. Twelve-year-old me just knew that she got choked up—but didn't cry—when it felt like her mother shut her down.

———

Mom had many one-liners that stuck with me over the years. She blurted these out without explanation and quickly moved on. I keep a small, running inventory of the ones that have stuck with me.

"Your grandfather was a sonofabitch as a father, but he was a pretty decent grandfather." Or, "Just be yourself" and "Marriage is hard work."

Later, when I was driving her to chemo, I told her she didn't have to worry about Dad, that we would take good care of him, and even move him up near us so he wouldn't be lonely.

"I just want you to know that your dad is selfish, and he'll take over your life if you let him," she said. She also said a version of this to my husband before she died. We'd shrugged it off at the time, but once Mom's absence asserted itself, Dad's presence began to smother just as she said it would.

Her "just be yourself" line has always been exceptionally vexing for me because I had no clue who "myself" was. I realize now how hard I was trying to conform to what I thought others wanted of me. My focus as an adopted child was more about trying not to make waves. As I try now to identify my feelings as an adolescent, the closest I can come is that I felt, well, numb. When Mom suggested I "be myself," I felt at a complete loss. Empty. How could I tell her I had no idea who I was? Would it have exasperated her even more? I wanted a reflection that mirrored my own to relate to, or, in the absence of that, to understand Mom's feelings in order to push against them to figure out what mine might have been. But Mom was stoic. She made pronouncements and moved on. I didn't ask questions and was provided little context.

Maybe she felt she was protecting me—from her difficult childhood, or from her struggles to individuate in the face of parenthood. By not sharing her feelings, she didn't allow me to help her through them or to understand them in contrast or in complement to mine. By taking it all on, I feel it was the beginning of a hot little ball of resentment within her.

Through it all—childhood, parenthood, chemotherapy—Mom said to me, "I just want you to be happy. I just want everything to be perfect." Was she modeling happiness, though? I had demons I hadn't even begun to recognize. I realize now how despondent she may have been. Instead of seeking out comfort, I absorbed her sadness and stress. There is no simile in that poem for a child who lives with sadness.

I understand now how conditional "if" is.

If a child lives with sadness, she learns to be . . .

I have not yet found the right word.

———

A few girls in my high school had "coming out" parties. I was not one of them, and I was not invited to any of their cotillions. But I heard about the champagne fountains and the white gowns and wondered why they were dressing like brides while I was home feeling lonely and rehearsing with the local orchestra. I went to my first cast party for the senior play—*Finian's Rainbow*—as a sophomore because my role as a violinist in the pit orchestra gave me enough dorkish agency to attend.

That night I learned the magical power of too many beers; French-kissed the leading man in his VW Bug; danced on the host's coffee table; and incurred Mom's wrath by coming home drunk at 2 a.m.

Me, fumbling with the keys at the front door, a bright light in the hallway and stumbling backward holding my hand over my face.

Mom: "How dare you! You're drunk. We'll talk about this tomorrow."

Me, stumbling toward my room in the dark, using the wall as support before heaving myself onto my bed: the room spinning. Me knocking the screen out of the casement window and vomiting into the backyard before passing out.

Tomorrow came and we didn't talk about it. Tension-filled silence and furrowed eyebrows conveyed the shame and humiliation I was supposed to feel as a result of what I had done. Was I expected to hang my head and feel guilt? Dad's contribution was, "So, I heard you had a few last night, eh?"

Mom heard about the coffee table dancing at work over the next few days. She was the head teller at our local bank. The drive-thru window was where she collected the cash and the gossip.

The bank's drive-thru window was made of thick, bulletproof glass tinted green and surrounded by polished stainless steel. The top tilted out and eased down at an angle to be almost flush with the building where the drawer swallowed your money or delivered your money. Feasibly, it was designed to bring the teller closer to her customers. I drove myself through many times to ask Mom for money for ice cream or before visiting the Burger King drive-thru, or just to check in; this was decades before cell phones.

I envied her efficiency as I watched her through the glass. She licked her thumb and counted out bills while stabbing the keys of the bank calculator with her index finger. She then gathered the money into a small pile, tapped it two or three times on its long side to level the bills, and put them into a white envelope that slid under a steel arm in the drive-thru drawer. With her hip or the heel of her hand, she pushed the drawer out to the window of the waiting car. Back then you had to push a button to talk to the teller.

"How would you like that, in twenties?" she might say. What I wanted to hear was "How are you doing today, honey?"

Behind that glass with her head down, she had the hardened expression that comes from concentration and working at a job she considered drudgery. I felt like I could see her frustration, but couldn't do anything to help her. When I had difficulty fitting in, or was teased for being overweight, or felt rejected by the popular kids, Mom buoyed me with the "just be yourself" line. She watched me struggle with my body image and identity. I had a sense that she knew my emotional pain intimately, even though I couldn't locate it yet myself, or even register that it was pain. I was used to not feeling anything at all.

———

My mother knew me by heart it seemed but gave me few clues as to who it was she was looking at, which made losing her acutely painful. I couldn't comprehend the questions I needed to ask her when she was alive, but they burst from me in the years after she died. I wanted to call her to ask for answers, but she was gone. Perhaps neither of us recognized ourselves in the other. The thing we shared was a shimmery pain that manifested itself in wholly different ways.

———

After Mom died of pancreatic cancer, I took another inventory of her bedroom—the closet, her dresser, the desk—deciding what to keep, what to donate, and what to throw away. I hadn't known Mom had considered The Hemlock Society, the right-to-die organization, until I found the brochure in her nightstand. I hadn't realized she'd been so religious until I found the rosary and the tiny bible in the same drawer. I looked in her jewelry box;

it was as if nothing had changed from my childhood. She'd kept everything we ever gave to her. I took the Shalimar bottle—its evaporated perfume now brown and gummed at the bottom. Inventorying her things magnified my feelings of loss and grief. It forced me to look at her in the way I felt I should have seen her when she was alive.

As I slid her clothes off their hangers, touching each of the dresses she wore throughout her sickness—cotton plaid muumuus she called her "organ friendly dresses"— I suggested we donate them. Dad had other plans. He commissioned memorial quilts with huge, garish daylilies (Mom's favorite flower) for each of us. The woman who sewed the quilts used her dress fabric to shape the petals and stems, but she used a crude, machined zig-zag stitch to attach them instead of the finer, appliqued hand technique Mom had skillfully practiced. Before she'd died, Mom had hand-quilted a bedspread for us as a wedding gift. She'd also hand-quilted wall hangings for my two sons.

Dad commissioned a memorial quilt for me. At his request, the woman machine-stitched "Consider the Lillies," which, had it been spelled correctly, was a favorite saying of Mom's. I hated that quilt, and I resented Dad for memorializing Mom during her sickness instead of celebrating her when she was healthy. Until a few years ago, he'd call me every year on the day of her death instead of on her birthday.

Back in her bedroom I took the framed poem off Mom's wall and hung it on mine.

————

"I know you love your father more than me," Mom said one day when we were alone in the kitchen. I was a teenager then. I denied it, but my denial sounded flat and untrue. The truth is, I didn't know how to love one parent more than the other so to be accused of feeling that way threw me. Dad was around less often, so it was easier to feel less watched. Mom was the enforcer, which made Dad's parenting job two-fold—mow the lawn and soak up his girls' positive attention.

I felt far from perfect. I didn't know how to please Mom or myself. Perfect seemed saved for the girls who had cotillions or dates to the senior prom. Only now do I realize she could have been talking about herself, their marriage, the burden of parenting that fell almost completely on her. No wonder the exasperation. As a parent myself now, I wish I could dial the phone to the past and ask, "How did you get through it with us?"

As an adult I now empathize with her. We could have had frank conversations. I could have asked her all of the questions I hadn't thought of yet.

Muffin Lane: The house we brought you home to.
Courtesy of Michael B. Culhane.

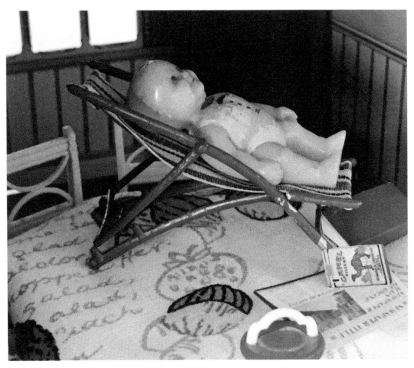

Gabriella. Your first baby photo (in your foster home).

The Blank Slate

By the time I decided to tell my parents about Ursula, I had already corresponded with her by phone and airmail, and we'd spent a weekend in New York City. She'd flown over from Scotland, where she worked as an administrator at an arts council. We'd walked by the former site of The Guild of the Infant Saviour.

All that meeting and communicating felt like I was doing something wrong; like I was cheating on my parents. I didn't want to hurt them by not telling them we'd met—if there's one thing adoptees hate above all it's secrets—but I also hadn't wanted to tell them because I thought it might hurt them.

My family was visiting my husband and me and our newborn son, in our first house in the rural village of Cambridge, New York. Mom and Dad were sitting in the living room. I went upstairs to get the watch fob Ursula had given me. She'd kept it, she said, because it was the heirloom of another family adoptee. She'd inherited it when her mother died and had saved it in case we ever met. Looking back, I'm unsure why I needed that object to tell my parents I'd met my birth mother, but I did. The child psychologist D. W. Winnicott would have called it a transitional object—a significant thing that serves as a stand-in for the mother, like a security blanket.

I sat in the middle of our secondhand couch, opened my fist, and placed the watch fob on the coffee table.

"I have something to tell you," I said, before breaking into sobs.

I blurted everything about finding my birth mother—the search, the airmail, the phone conversations, and meeting her in person. In my mind I can bring myself back to that couch and the way I felt—desperate and crying—the betrayer. I was wrong.

Mom had an innate sense of me. I realize now that she knew me better than anyone. I was also wrong that finding Ursula would close a circle for me and answer all my questions, or perhaps get me closer to a truth I could call my own. I didn't yet have the words to describe all my feelings. Things still felt fragile—like the residue of a story that was chalk dust. If someone were to blow on it, my past would be gone.

I looked up, still heaving; to see if my parents were enraged, or worse, would cut me off.

"Is that it? Is that all?" Mom said. "For a minute I was worried sick you were going to tell us you had cancer or something."

———

Two years later, here is what Mom ate once a day, every day after being diagnosed with pancreatic cancer.

Aminosyn II 10%	40 GM	Sodium Chloride	140 MEQ
Dextrose 70%	175 GM	Potassium Acetate	20 MEQ
Lyposyn III 20%	25 GM	Potassium Chloride	40 MEQ
Water for inject	120 ML	Calcium Gluconate	10 MEQ
Sodium Phosphate	10 MMOL	Magnesium Sulfate	10 MEQ
Sodium Acetate	20 MEQ	Trace Minerals	3M

Infuse 3:1 IV over 13 hours daily, just prior to infusion, add 10 ML MVI, 2 ML (20 MG) Pepcid and 1 ML (500 MG) Ascorbic Acid to TPN bag. Spike bag with tubing and purge all air just prior to hookup. Infuse XXX AIM pump, program pump, infuse XXX 1000 ML: Taper up: 01:00 (hr:min) KVO: XXX 04:00 (hr:min) Store in refrigerator, do not freeze.

Dad prepared Mom's TPN bag every night—TPN stood for *total parenteral nutrition.* He injected various syringes of medicine and other nutrients prescribed for someone with inoperable cancer through the ports in what looked like a gallon-sized Ziploc bag and then kneaded the bag like bread, dispersing the nutrients into a creamy liquid that resembled baby formula. Mom called this "her dinner" and spent the last year and a half of her life on this liquid diet.

Each night Dad cleaned and flushed the port in Mom's chest. He pressed the air bubbles out of the bag and then hung it on a rolling IV trolley. Mom watched TV with us, did her nightly knitting, and walked slowly around the house before dragging the entire contraption to bed with her. The liquid dripped slowly into her veins throughout the night. By mid-morning it was gone, and she could disconnect the apparatus again until that night, when the process repeated.

Every day, until she couldn't anymore, Mom rose early to make Dad breakfast and lunch before sending him off to work. It made me furious. He should be the one caring for her by taking care of himself, I'd thought. I could have been more empathetic. Dad *was* caring for Mom. As the former chief of the volunteer fire department in our hometown, he'd earned EMT-IV status. His ability to inject medicine was one of the reasons she'd been allowed to stay at home. Sure she made his breakfast, lunch, and dinner, but he prepared her meals too: every night in those TPN bags.

Mom made her peace with this routine. In fact, she depended on it. She was the caretaker of our family, and in the end, I felt it brought her solace to attend to our needs for as long as she could.

"I don't want your Dad sitting around here moping over me," she said. "I want him to be able to take his mind off things until he can't anymore."

"Don't talk like that, Mom," I said.

"Well, it's true," she said. "You need to have a wedding on the same day as my funeral because your father needs someone to take care of him."

Dad tried to spoil Mom in that last year with material things. He tried to buy her a Mercedes convertible she'd never expressed any interest in having; "I'm not going to parade around town in that thing, Michael," she'd said.

Mom got a urinary catheter for Christmas that year, and a hospital bed in the middle of the living room. Dad gave her a platinum band with diamonds that she refused to wear for practical reasons (it didn't fit her emaciated fingers, and she said it was too showy for someone with advanced cancer.) After she died, I wore it for a time as part of my wedding set before I got divorced.

After she died, Dad bought and traded in at least four different vehicles ranging from a full-size, dual-wheel, king cab, 4x4 pickup truck, to a two-seater Honda convertible we joked he needed a crowbar to get in and out of.

He was full of grief and desperately lonely.

———

One February, I drove down to Williamsburg, Virginia, to help care for Mom. Sometimes major sickness allows for more vulnerability and openness. I thought cancer might soften us both. I thought, perhaps, she would impart all her motherly wisdom on me seeing as I was a new mother. Our second son, Sam, had been born just a few weeks before the exploratory surgery that had diagnosed Mom's cancer. But pain hardens people, and shame, grief, and fear conspired to keep us at a comfortable, uncomfortable distance.

"I can't believe it's come to this, that my daughter has to do these things for me," she said one day as I emptied the warm amber piss out of her catheter bag and into the toilet.

"It's okay, Mom," I said. "I'm happy to do it."

She sighed. A muscle flexed in her jaw. I knew she wasn't happy to have it done.

I was there to drive her to her last chemotherapy appointment and assure her we'd take care of Dad. "Your Dad will take over your life if you let him," she said.

I was there to program the clock on the stove to buzz at fifteen-minute intervals so I could press her morphine drip. Mom spent her days mostly unconscious in what we called her morphine coma. If we didn't dispense the medication four times an hour, the pain would overwhelm her and wake her up. I'd made a mistake once of missing a few fifteen-minute windows before coming up with the idea of using the kitchen timer. Perhaps I'd been lost in my work, or simply gazing out the window having lost track of time, but when I went into her bedroom she was writhing and crumpled on the floor next to her hospital bed. I pressed the morphine button immediately and helped her back into bed; the heft of her emaciated body surprised me, as did the force of her remaining strength.

"No one should ever have to experience pain like this," she said as the morphine took hold. I wonder now if that was the last thing she ever said to me.

I was there to hold her left hand when she died early that late February morning, and I was the one to call her hospice nurse, Janni, and then the coroner, who took her body out the front door, down the brick steps, and into the misty, chilly Virginia pre-dawn.

And then, she wasn't there.

———

Losing my mother introduced me to a bottomless grief that resurfaces even now, decades after her death. The grief takes many forms. Mom had been my rock, my protector. She'd also been tightly wound, practical, and exasperated. Looking back, I felt I'd wasted many years not asking her the questions I'd wanted answers to about my adoption, or about her as a person and not a mother or a wife. I didn't even know what I didn't know yet and she'd died so young at fifty-five. I am fifty-four this year and she's nearly twenty-five years gone. I mark those years by the ages of my children.

The morning of her diagnosis was the first time Mom held Sam. He and I had flown to Richmond, Virginia, barely two weeks after I'd given birth. My cesarean scar was so fresh it was weeping pus and I leaked breast milk all over my shirt as I sobbed openly on the plane rocking Sam tightly against my chest. We got to the hospital just in time for Mom to hold him in pre-op. She was lying flat with all the catheters and tubes in place. She held Sam's little body and lifted him up over her head. "He's perfect," she said.

The surgeon said he was 95 percent sure they wouldn't find any cancer. He said the surgery would take hours, so we waited at a home nearby. Dad went out for lunch. I stayed behind and nursed Sam.

The phone call came much earlier than expected. I answered the phone attached to the wall. "It's unresectable," the surgeon said. "I give her six months."

Dad returned from lunch. I had to deliver the news.

We saw Mom in her hospital room later, holding a pillow over the giant wound in her open stomach—they'd opened her up from her pubic bone to her rib cage. She was stoic.

"The next time you come, Michael, bring me the checkbook," she said. "I need to balance it."

———

It wasn't my first experience with cancer. My cousin Karen was eighteen when she died of leukemia after a bone marrow transplant—she'd been one of the first people to receive what was then a wholly experimental treatment. Cancer was everywhere in my adoptive parent's medical history. I would find out later from Ursula that pancreatic cancer had also killed her father, and I began to worry what form of cancer might be ticking inside me.

Dad had been invoking the "C" word since he was in his mid-fifties (the age his mother died from complications of diabetes and alcoholism). "I don't know how much time I have left, Meggie," he'd say.

He was 80 in January.

When I reported my relatives' cancers and various other diseases—checking off all the boxes in all the waiting rooms of all the doctor's offices for all my annual physicals and hospitalizations—it never occurred to me that our biology didn't belong together and that their medical history was not mine. Before I'd met my birth mother, I'd effectively had no medical history simply because I hadn't known it.

I was once removed. I was adopted.

———

When Ursula and I first met she'd promised to "be my open book" and to answer all my questions. "Ask me anything," she'd said. So I did.

Because she had invited these questions, I felt justified asking: "Who was my father?" "Why did your parents send you away to have me?" "Weren't you mad at your mother for sending you away?" "If it was legal at the time would I have been an abortion?"

I have never been able to get what I felt were straight answers out of my parents or Ursula about my adoption. The absence of clear answers felt like everyone was keeping secrets from me. Within days of me telling her about the publication of this book, Ursula sent me a congratulatory card. She wrote a certified letter days later in which she refused to grant me permission to use photos she'd given me (one of which was of our reunion) without first being able to read, revise, and make changes to my entire manuscript. Why? Did she feel she had something to hide or be ashamed of? In the past Ursula had denied feeling any shame or trauma. She called them "useless emotions."

I began to wonder if my adoptive grandparents and Ursula conspired to hide the truth to protect future me from it. As I uncovered details there were so many intersections between both families that it seemed my adoption could have been engineered rather than left to chance. I pieced together stories fueled by bits of fact that I then embroidered with my imagination. Mom died before I could formulate the more profound questions I'd needed to ask. I like to think she would have told me the unvarnished truth because she was straightforward and practical, but she'd died so young that I also wonder if I've martyred her in my memories.

Soon the questions outweighed the answers, and the answers begged more questions. I found myself stuck in a vortex of circular reasoning and a priori theories.

Meanwhile, Ursula was getting sick of my questions. She snapped at me during a visit to our house. Over dinner, she'd said, "That's it, you're cut off."

"Cut off from what?" I said.

"No more stories, no more tape recording. It's an invasion of my privacy," she said.

"Invasion," her husband Frank repeated in his thick Scottish accent smacking the table with his open hand.

"Whose memoir are you writing anyway: yours or mine?" she said. I was shocked and hurt. I felt betrayed. I shut down.

Why were my questions an invasion? She'd promised to be my open book. I'd barely filled in the blanks. Had I hit a particularly tender nerve? Why now? I mean, with her permission I'd tape-recorded many of our cocktail conversations. She'd seen me taking notes. She knew I was writing everything down.

"I can't write your memoir," I told her. "This is my story."

Maybe I was picking at the scabs of wounds she'd thought had healed long ago. Maybe my line of questioning caught her off guard. Perhaps she felt badgered by the unassailable and sometimes unanswerable question all children ask of their parents, "Why?"

Shame, I've learned, is spring-loaded.

———

Ursula told me she'd been reading about the Blank Slate theory. Developed by philosopher John Locke in the seventeenth century, it held that a baby was born void of any prior information or history. The Blank Slate theory made perfect sense when overlaid with adoption. Who wouldn't want a baby ready to be imprinted by whatever nurturing adult it came into contact with? Prospective parents were likely sold on the idea that we were Play-Doh ready to be molded by our environment. Until the theory was debunked, its proponents included most of the major institutions of science and education, the Catholic Church, and the criminal justice system.

This theory discounted the nature side of nature/nurture. In his book *The Blank Slate: The Modern Denial of Human Nature,* Harvard psychologist Steven Pinker said modern science invalidates the three major tenets of the Blank Slate theory: that the mind has no innate traits; that people are born good and corrupted by society; and that each of us has a soul that makes choices free from biology. The term for this comes from British philosopher Gilbert Ryle: "the ghost in the machine."

Ursula seemed to cast me as a ghost in the machine, born pure and corrupted by other forces, not by her. This played itself out in our conversations as I was trying to get to know her.

"When I was in high school and all through college, I was bulimic," I told her when we met in New York the first time.

"Oh, you didn't get that from me," she said.

This would become her catchphrase anytime I felt like she heard me describe something vulnerable about myself that she didn't find likable. She would repeat the phrase each time I tried to offer up a piece of myself to find out more about her.

"I've struggled with bouts of terrible depression," I said.

"You didn't get that from me."

Without realizing it, Ursula was invalidating both her existence and mine. It felt like she was selectively pointing out the pieces of me that weren't pieces of her—which, according to the Blank Slate theory, was all of the pieces. It was maddening. I had hoped that finding my birth mother meant closing in on what made me tick, finding out parts of myself, trying to assemble the "whole." Ursula, it seemed, was deflecting every piece of me that I flung at her.

The idea that a baby was a social construct and not a biological one was so laughable that it seemed to be an argument for the Virgin birth.

The '60s presented an interesting paradox for women. As much as it seemed women were awakening culturally, socially, and sexually, there was also an absurd divide.

Women were beginning to work outside the home, demand equal pay for equal work, and break down the double standard that only men could have premarital sex; yet women remained repressed. The Sexual Revolution was in full swing, but it had been an entirely different kind of revolution for unwed mothers.

The pill was legal, but in 1964 it was still unavailable in eight states. Pope John XXIII formed a commission that issued its report in the year of my birth proposing "artificial birth control was not intrinsically evil and that Catholic [married] couples should be allowed to decide for themselves about the methods to be employed." But his successor, Pope Paul VI, rejected it.

It's doubtful Ursula had access to the pill given her Catholic upbringing. Combine the Blank Slate theory with the vicious moral fight over the pill, and the idea of "mother" (more specifically the unwed mother) could be reduced to a definition that meant little more than the human vessel for carrying a baby.

————

The poem "Children Learn What They Live" came packaged inside containers of Enfamil in the '60s—this was the poem Mom had kept framed and hung over her dresser. The poem passively reinforced the power of nurture over nature. I could almost hear the caseworkers sharing the Blank Slate theory with the girls at The Guild of the Infant Saviour. I understood why they might have thought it could provide a balm for unwed mothers who were expected to surrender their children. The caseworkers and Catholic Charities were trying to help them find a way to make that renunciation palatable. But what translated in hindsight (what they were learning and living) was "the mother does not matter."

Unwed mothers could be washed clean by the act of relinquishing their babies: We were born so that they could be born again.

————

My adoptive parents had lived little over a mile from Ursula and her family in Norwalk, Connecticut. Their first home, the one they brought me home to, was a Colonial house with clapboard siding. It had been the original farmhouse on a cul-de-sac that was purchased by my grandfather. Pop Pop had bought the swath of land, moved the house, and it became a small development of homes on a dead-end road that was quiet and safe. He named the street Muffin Lane after Dad's youngest sister, Mary.

The man who designed and patented the modern stapler and staple remover at the E. H. HOTCHKISS COMPANY once owned the house. Fridolin Polzer died there in 1963 at the age of eighty-four according to the *New York Times*. I wonder if he knew how much was held together by the house now or how I'd revisited it with Dad nearly forty years later with new eyes. On our visit I'd seen the heart he made in the cement when he and Mom poured the new foundation. Inside the outline of the heart he'd scratched "Mike & Bert" with what was likely the tip of a nail. The woman who owned the place said she'd always wondered if it was two men who'd been in love.

"No," Dad said. "No. That was my Roberta."

I'd had my first birthday in that house, a swing set in the backyard and a swing in the living room. I remember our living room decorated with Christmas lights and the sounds of the Mormon Tabernacle Choir playing on the turntable.

Ursula told me that her mother used to play bridge with Mom-Mops, my adopted grandmother: Dad's mother.

Had my grandparents known Ursula was pregnant at the same time my parents were pining for a baby? Had Ursula's mother confided in Mom-Mops?

My grandfather (Pop Pop) had a best friend from high school who had become the powerful bishop of the Bridgeport Catholic Diocese, Bishop (Walter) Curtis. Dad told me Bishop Curtis used to come to their house to play bridge. He'd overheard the two of them laughing in the other room and remembers the Bishop said,

"You know, Frank, I like to cheat." Dad told me he'd also overheard the Bishop say, "The only object is to win."

"They were always laughing like hell," Dad said. "They were two Irish jokers."

Dad had been a seminarian at St. Thomas, a school overseen by Curtis, before meeting Mom. He told me Bishop Curtis had helped facilitate my adoption. "It got us to the top of the list at least," he said.

When the stories of Catholic priest sex abuse began to receive widespread attention in the 1990s, it was Bishop Curtis and the Bridgeport Diocese that came under some of the most intense scrutiny for widespread sexual abuse. Curtis knew of the violations and had willfully ignored the issues for years, refusing to remove pedophile priests—which allowed them to continue abusing their victims—then re-assigning some to other parishes instead of dealing with the crimes. He destroyed complaint records and stated publicly that he didn't believe pedophilia was a permanent condition. Most of the victims were between the ages of five and eighteen, and most of the abuses happened when Curtis led the diocese.

It was reported that "the single gravest moral and legal lapse was the consistent practice of Bishops Lawrence Shehan, Walter Curtis, and Edward Egan—over four decades—of leaving abusive priests in service, and thereby making it possible for them to continue committing abusive acts."

Curtis went to his death never disclosing what he knew or admitting what he'd done. He was cancer within a closed system.

Had something terrible happened to my Dad at St. Thomas? Had Bishop Curtis helped facilitate my adoption as a way of buying his silence?

Mom-Mops had been an obstetric nurse. One day she'd said to Dad, "When you get married, the first child you have comes anytime—the second one takes nine months."

What did that mean? Had Mom-Mops known of Ursula's pregnancy, or was she being a benevolent mother? Had they helped Ursula's parents financially to send her to The Guild of the Infant Saviour? Had Pop Pop used his influence to maneuver the Bishop on my parents' behalf? Was it typical for Catholic Charities to have placed me with them so quickly after my parents had been married?

———

I was blessed in the church of St. Thomas the Apostle on November 4, 1966. I never went to catechism or took communion. The imprimatur on my Certificate of Blessing of An Adopted Child is Walter W. Curtis, S.T.D., Bishop of Bridgeport.

———

Ursula's email said she was re-doing her will. She asked me to call her ASAP with my Social Security number. I hadn't talked to her since our Christmas phone call three months previous, which was a few months after she'd told me I was "cut off."

I couldn't know the reason for her sudden phone call, but we'd maintained a stoic silence about her outburst on her last visit. I'd also told her then that I'd been accepted to Bennington to get my MFA in writing. She'd been sitting in the wingback chair in our living room with a copy of *Harper's Magazine* held up to her face. She moved the magazine down slowly so I could see her eyes over the top of it.

"I suppose they accept everyone who can pay the tuition," she said.

She licked her finger and flipped through a few more pages before setting the magazine on her lap and ripping out a page. It was an ad for "The Great Courses," a multi-CD tutorial on story writing that cost $99. She handed it to me.

"Here," she'd said, "why put your family into debt to chase your passion? It seems selfish."

———

I'd read that if you don't deal with unexpressed anger it could lead to cancer. I couldn't bring myself to openly talk with Ursula about my feelings, so I'd pushed them down, and they festered into a repressed, furious ball. I couldn't understand why my biological mother couldn't empathize with her daughter's natural curiosity about her childhood. Isn't that what daughters do, badger their mothers for answers? How had my line of questioning, which I thought was utterly normal, offended her? It felt like she was slamming the promised open book shut in my face. Why the unexpected email to call her with such haste? I worried she was calling to tell me that she was writing me out of her will.

I got around to calling her a day and a half later. "How are you?" I asked.

"I have uterine cancer," she said.

"I guess if I'm going to have cancer, this is the one to have," she said. "They just liquefy your lady parts and suck them through your twat."

I grimaced on the other end of the phone. Ursula said it twice more: "Twat." "Twat."

I wanted to tell her to cut it out, to which she would likely have replied, "Exactly."

"Have they staged it yet?" I asked. Staging cancer means assigning a number (1 to 4) that correlates with the severity of the diagnosis. If a patient is at Stage 1, chances for recovery are good. Stage 4, which was the stage Mom was when they found her pancreatic cancer, meant you were pretty much fucked.

They hadn't staged it yet.

"At least it's not lung or stomach cancer," she said, "because I like to smoke and eat."

A week or so later, when I'd allowed myself to absorb the information, I googled "uterine cancer staging." I found that the lungs, lymph nodes, liver, and bones are the spaces into which this type of cancer typically moves.

Ursula's womb had been the tiny apartment I'd rented for nine months. With my adoptive mother dead now for about eighteen years, Ursula was the only mother figure I had left. Now she was sick, and I was sick with worry for her, but I was also wracked with feelings of selfishness thinking she might take my entire life story to the grave.

———

What scared me most when I first met Ursula was that I would be unable to connect with her in a mother-daughter bonding way that most adoptees hope for. I didn't know then about attachment disorder. I hadn't yet understood my struggles with intimacy and how they dovetailed with my adoption. I worried that our wounds were covered in a particular kind of scar tissue that per-haps even honesty couldn't pierce. My search for her had started because I'd wanted to understand her story and the how and why she'd come to let me go.

After meeting her I began to question if the Blank Slate theory didn't have some merits.

My parents, through nurture perhaps, seemed to have sanded off the sharper edges of the personality I saw in Ursula. She admitted she'd likely not have been a good mother, but I'd long questioned if she believed that or if she believed it because that's what the caseworkers likely said to the young women relinquishing their babies.

These narratives are born out when I read books like *The Girls Who Went Away*, by Ann Fessler. The book is a collection of oral histories of birth mothers who were sent away to unwed mothers' homes in the years before Roe v. Wade. In it are repeated refrains of what the birth mothers said they heard from the caseworkers or the nuns. These sayings seem designed to undercut biology and the mother-infant bond:

"You've got nothing to offer him/her."

"The baby will do better in a home where they can properly take care of him/her."

"It's for his/her own good."

————

A Blank Slate implies a clean slate, but there is no cleanness in a system that pretends to play God; in caseworkers thinking they know what's best for a child when nature and intuition justify that a baby stay with its mother. In conceiving and using the theory that a baby is a blank slate it implies that the slate needs to be cleansed, that some sort of escape must happen, that mother and baby must be freed of their dirty past, unburdened of shame, secrets, loss, and grief.

There is no getting free from trauma, and most times that trauma isn't ours to carry.

I have spent a lifetime chasing down the emotions being adopted was meant to absolve me of—low self-esteem, feelings of unworthiness, deep shame, grief, and a sense of profound loss. I read about inherited trauma, which is sometimes called intergenerational trauma relating to the biological field of study called epigenetics. Suffering can be transferred from first generation survivors to second-generation offspring and beyond. It can manifest in ways that are baffling to the sufferer until a genealogical context is understood.

———

In his book *It Didn't Start with You,* Mark Wolynn writes, "The history you share with your family begins before you are even conceived . . . that means that before your mother was even born, your mother, your grandmother, and the earliest traces of you were all in the same body—three generations sharing the same biological environment."

I realized I had huge gaps in my emotional language. While trying to write about my experiences, I was pressed by my mentor, Joan Wickersham, to describe what I'd been feeling during my childhood. I struggled hard to identify a feeling—any feeling—and finally wrote back that I couldn't identify anything: all I remembered was being numb.

"Numbness *is* a feeling," she said.

Wolynn uses exercises and questions to help his patients identify words that relate to underlying, intergenerational trauma. I call this *naming* the feeling before *understanding* the feeling. Words have a way of giving permission. Once I'd identified numbness as a feeling, out crawled shame, grief, fear of abandonment, and loneliness, among others. It was up to me to confront these feelings and heal.

Wolynn writes that trauma words like these are what he calls "non-declarative memory." Once they're identified he overlays a person's words with genealogical and cultural context, like a puzzle.

Survivors of the surviving victims of the Holocaust, for example, may have suicidal ideation that manifests itself in the form of thoughts such as, "I see myself burning and flying away in smoke and ash." Generations of Black Americans carry trauma from the effects of slavery, systemic racism, and police violence; as do refugees from political persecution, diaspora, and migration.

For adoptees, intergenerational trauma manifests as, among other things, unresolved grief, dissociation, shame, attachment disorder, and distrust. In short, we question our right to exist.

"An infant's primary currency is a mother's focused attention," writes Wollyn. "When her focus is steadfast, the child feels ecstatic and wealthy. When her attention is inconsistent or disengaged, a child experiences a form of emotional bankruptcy. These early experiences of getting a lot or not enough can forge a blueprint for how much we let ourselves receive later in life."

I suppose I came to my adoptive parents as a half-vacant vessel—wary of the world—appraising it silently and at all times instead of interacting with it and letting my feelings be known. In hindsight, I wonder if I'd wiped my own slate clean by trying to conform and contort myself into the image others wanted me to reflect. Had I put myself in a box? Had I erased myself?

Locke's theory undermined heredity entirely, and yet a few pieces resonate with me, particularly that "ideas are grounded in experience, which varies from person to person, differences of opinion arise not because one mind is equipped to grasp the truth and another is defective, but because the two minds have had different histories." I've wrestled with these sentences, particularly because Ursula and I have two minds, two different histories, and two different versions of my birth and embodied identity.

Even William Godwin, one of the founders of liberal political philosophy, echoed the idea of the blank slate when he wrote, "Children are a sort of raw material put into our hands," and their minds are "like a sheet of white paper."

Godwin's only daughter was born from his marriage to Mary Wollstonecraft, who was considered the "mother of feminism." She was pregnant before they married, and they wed to "legitimize" the baby. Mary died of complications from the birth just ten days after her daughter was born. Their daughter Mary Shelley authored the literary classic *Frankenstein,* which is the story of Victor Frankenstein, who creates a monster from sewn-together body parts, which he animates to life. Wandering the woods after having endured rejection and retaliation from those who are frightened by him, Frankenstein's monster learns to read via the notebooks and letters of his creator so he can understand his "adopted" family.

———

I remember the slate chalkboards of my school days and how they showed vestiges of what had been written there before. The chalk dust becomes smudged across the board, creating faint white lines that remain like a ghostly history of lessons learned. The erased dust collects in the wooden eraser holder. In some cases "blank slate" translates more literally to "erased slate," but erasure implies something existed before and it had to be wiped clean, which negates the argument altogether.

In computer science the term "ghost in the machine" is used to explain when a program runs counter to its intended expectation. I began to wonder if I was the ghost in the machine—the one gumming up everyone's comfortable narrative by questioning my origin story.

———

Many proponents of adoption marketed infant children as blank slates: spotless minds. Worse, in the nineteenth century, foundlings and illegitimate children could be absolved of their sins (of being born out of wedlock) by being adopted into a legitimized family.

I could project how I might have turned out had Ursula raised me. Of course I'd have been different, but who is to know what Gabriella Herman could have been capable of since I was never that girl. She is locked away; a number on a piece of paper in a vast archive of other papers in a system that assigns and erases adoptee identity.

She is closed in a musty book in the New York Public Library.

She is Schrödinger's cat—both dead and alive—which allows me to write about her in the third person and in both the present and past tense.

I didn't want to find out after Ursula was dead that what she'd told me had all just been a terrific story. Worse, I didn't want to be left with two dead mothers and one dead-end story.

I asked her on the phone how it all started; the cancer, that is.

"I started bleeding," she said.

Which, I suppose, is how it begins and ends for us women.

Gabriella. Your first baby photo (in your foster home). Courtesy of the author.

You in your high chair at Grammy's house. Forest Street, Norwalk, CT.

Other Names for Home*

Almshouse; American Female Guardian Society and Home for the Friendless; Association for Befriending Children and Young Girls; Colored Orphan Asylum; Door of Hope; Female Employment Society; Foundling Asylum of the Sisters of Charity; Girl's Town; Guardian Angel Home; Half Orphan Asylum for Destitute and Abandoned Children; Hebrew Orphan Asylum; Home for Fallen Women; Home for Friendless Women & Children; House of Another Chance; Home for Friendless Females or Children; Home for Idiotic, Feebleminded, Paralytic & Deformed Children & Adults; House of Industry; Industrial School Association; Magdalene Home; Mercy Train; New England Home for Little Wanderers; New York Foundling Hospital; Orphan Train; Queen of the Rosary Motherhouse; Randall's Island; Sheltering Arms; Sisters of Charity; Society for the Relief of Half-Orphan and Destitute Children; Society for the Relief of Respectable Aged Indigent Females;

*Curated from a list of names in *Adoption Agencies, Orphanages, and Maternity Homes: An Historical Directory,* bound loose-leaf binder, pages: 230–62; covering New York city's five boroughs. Irma and Paul Milstein Division of United States History, Local History and Genealogy, New York Public Library.

Soldiers' Orphan Schools; Sorrowful Mother Home; St. Agatha Home for Children; St. Mary's Temporary Shelter for Unmarried Mothers; St. Vincent's Female Orphan Asylum; The House of Providence; The Guild of the Infant Saviour.

You in your high chair at Grammy's house on Forest Street, Norwalk, CT. Courtesy of Michael B. Culhane.

Your flower-sniffing expression

Mother's Day

It's ironic that the flowers my mother loved so much were daylilies. They were weedy and spread like disease. She transplanted them from our childhood home in Connecticut to Williamsburg, Virginia, where they bloomed and she died.

Throughout a two-year struggle with pancreatic cancer, the daylilies were her strength.

She planted her garden and cultivated it with hybrid varieties, including one named after me: Megan's Love. Mom and I laughed that it was our family plot and that someday she'd be pushing them up through the springtime soil. It was part of the gallows humor we shared during her illness. It got us through.

One day, I saw Mom had hung a Ziggy cartoon on the refrigerator, beneath a magnet that said: "Quilter's Keep You in Stitches." The cartoon featured Ziggy standing under a rainbow holding daisies. It read, "Today is a gift, that's why they call it the present."

It was one of the things I kept after she died.

———

I spent the month of February that year in Williamsburg. Out of vacation days at work, I had been allowed to take my laptop, hostel at our kitchen table, and work whenever I could. I wrote science stories and news releases while Mom lay in a morphine-induced sleep in the hospital bed we had planted in the living room. In many ways, I feel I did my best work there.

She slept, nearly unmoving, for most of the day, with IV morphine in her left arm. When the pain verged on overwhelming, she pressed a button for more morphine. We called it her morphine coma. I didn't think she could hear anything, but once when I was deep into writing she said, "If this is what heaven is like, it won't be so bad: You tapping away at your computer. . . . I could handle that."

We had never talked about her death. Not really. Of course, it had been the elephant in the room ever since the doctors had given her six months to live. So I asked her: "How will we know you're 'in,' Mom? Heaven, I mean. We need to figure out a sign you can send us when you're 'in.' Maybe you could move something around the house, maybe levitate it, or knock it to the floor, push something off the counter. We need to agree on this, so we'll know you're okay."

———

There was nothing in bloom that late February in Williamsburg. Everything was brown and wilted, and the thick stench of the West Point paper mill was as heavy in the air as lacquer. After she died, we had a wake and a full open-casket funeral, even though Mom had told us we were free to just "put her in a baggie by the side of the road." We returned from Mom's funeral in a cold drizzle. Dad had picked the flowers—Stargazer lilies. It was a romantic gesture on his part, and none of us had the heart to tell him that she had always considered Stargazers "stinky" and "toady." She never could abide fuss, especially fuss over her.

Hospice had organized an array of food for us at the house so we wouldn't have to worry about anything. Mom's nurse, Janni, was there for much-needed hugs and to remind me to eat something.

———

My parents' kitchen overlooked the screened-in porch and Mom's daylily garden. I looked out through the drizzle, and there was a rainbow—a corny Ziggy rainbow. I stood gazing out over her garden and her browned lilies. It was her sign. She was "in." We didn't have to worry anymore. I ate something.

———

It was devastating for my father, living in the house that spring. The daylilies pushed themselves through the earth, and he felt trapped—surrounded by vibrant, living reminders of Mom. I returned to Williamsburg to uproot Mom's lilies and replant them in my garden so they could bloom where my family was planted.

I still maintain what I call the family plot. My mother's daylily is a delicate, buttery yellow with frilly edges; Dad's lily is a maroon flower with tiny, vibrant lime pistils; my grandmother's flower is a stalwart magenta with a lemon-colored throat.

I mark every season by their rebirth, and each summer morning by the fistfuls of cocoon-like blooms that burst open and turn their colorful faces to the sun.

Your flower-sniffing expression.
Courtesy Michael B. Culhane.

Daddy, 1966

O' Father Where Art Thou

He was my father, or so I am told. He was twenty-three years old when I was born. White, from an English background, graduated high school, went on to a two-year technical college, and lived one town over from Ursula, in Ridgefield, Connecticut. He was an electrician's mate in the Navy, and she told me his name was Dick Sanford. Ursula listed his physical particulars on my non-identifying information like this: 6'5" 200 lbs., big frame, blue eyes, blond hair, fair skin.

She could have been describing my two sons.

I can't say I cared who my biological father was. He seemed ancillary to my life. I admit to being fascinated by the motherhood aspect of my adoption, mostly because motherhood was something Ursula and I shared in different ways. She was not motherly in the least and yet she was my mother by trade, having done the physical labor of having me. My focus had been on trying to understand the whys of how a mother surrenders a baby. Not in a judgmental way, in a questioning way. I was interested in the mechanics of surrender.

But as I got to know Ursula I realized I wasn't going to be getting any concrete answers from her. My birth father became the next logical piece of the puzzle. Interestingly, there was no mechanism with Catholic Charities to search for a birth father. What I knew was a) I had a father and b) according to Ursula, it could have been anyone. Therein lies another paradox. How do you search for someone who could be anyone?

I thought about how to begin such a search and figured the best place to start would be with the name Ursula gave me before she began to backpedal: before she offered up "anyone."

One day I sat down at my laptop and typed in the following search parameters: Dick Sanford, Richard Sanford, Dick Sanford Navy 1966, Dick Sanford Ridgefield Connecticut. My little search, which started innocently enough, turned into a sort of fantasy football league for fathering.

As you might expect, there were many Richard Sanfords. One guy was the Director of Space Initiatives Global Defense, Space & Security Group at Cisco Systems, Inc. He looked dweeby in his corporate picture, especially with the prescription glasses that looked as though the lenses had half-darkened in the sun. Neither Ursula nor I would have found him attractive, and I ruled him out.

There was Richard Sanford the writer whose bio proclaimed, "He has made his living as a short order cook, computer programmer, and freelance writer. He has owned a pizza restaurant with another aspiring writer while serving as an editor of a small press in the pizza empire of Chicago."

This guy was attractive and good looking in a way I had always found intriguing: clear, tender eyes, slightly balding, open, honest face tinged with a hint of tortured writer. His black and white photo showed him with his head quizzically tilted in that way writers tilt their heads, as if to convey brooding intellectuality. This guy had possibilities, but I saw no physical resemblance, and no mention of the Navy. Plus, he was too young. I ruled him out.

I went down a deep Google rabbit hole and felt I was getting closer. There was a Dick Sanford in Napa Valley who seemed promising. His photo showed him to be tall and good-looking in a Paul Newman way. He seemed to have swagger if you can tell such a thing from a picture (you can). In the photo, he wore Levi's, a light pink button-down, and an embossed leather belt. He had bright blue eyes rimmed with a darker blue, and a broad smile that creased the corners of his eyes. His straight white teeth and his pose (leaning forward with his left arm resting on his left leg with a glass of wine in his right hand) reminded me of someone at ease with himself. Traits I would ascribe to myself on a day when I felt good about my body.

This Dick Sanford was a sommelier, or rather the owner of Alma Rosa Winery and Vineyards. The wine staff had had a guest-starring role in the movie *Sideways*, and their wines had also been featured in *The Kids Are Alright*. This guy had it together in a way that made me want him to be my birth father (he'd been elected to the Vintners Hall of Fame!). His wife, Thekla, in her picture, had a similar build to both Ursula and me. She was solid and authoritative looking with a thin-lipped smile. She was wearing a white T-shirt, a chunky turquoise necklace, and a jean jacket. I took this as a sign that he liked women of our type, temperament, and build. Coupled with the fact that his bio said he served in Vietnam in the Navy, I took this to be very encouraging. I began to fantasize about life on a Napa Valley vineyard with my handsome father, cool stepmother (with whom I would, of course, bond immediately) and unlimited Pinot Noir. I let myself ride the fantasy until I scrolled down to the part in his bio where he graduated from Cal-Berkeley in 1965. He was immediately drafted into the Navy and served in the war until 1968. Wrong coast, wrong time frame, case closed, fantasy sunk. Not my father.

The story I'd convinced myself of since I heard the name Sanford and father in the same sentence goes like this: My best friend in high school was a Sanford. We grew up a quarter mile from each other in West Redding, Connecticut. It was a town her relatives helped found. There was a street called Sanford Town Road. I imagined she had an Uncle Dick who lived in Ridgefield. As the imaginary pieces of this puzzle fit together, I wondered if she and I had been cousins all along. That would explain so much, I told myself, like how we were close as sisters. Inseparable. I began telling people that this could, in fact, be the case. How crazy would it be to find out that my best friend in high school was really my cousin? There were so many ways in which this story could be correct; the dates line up, Dick Sanford lived one town over in Ridgefield, the Sanford family was influential to the founding of Redding. In telling this story, it got more plausible each time. I could see how Ursula's stories could materialize as real over the course of years of her recounting them. The more I kept repeating this story as a possibility, the more concrete it felt to me until I mustered the gumption to message my friend.

"Hey, I've had a story in my head . . . ," I wrote.

"LOL, nope. Can't be. I don't have any uncles named Dick," she wrote back.

Case opened. Case closed. Wrong story. Not my father.

There were two Dick Sanfords I thought might be very close to the guy who could be my birth father. When asked to describe him again, Ursula said, "Oh, I couldn't even conjure his face now. I remember he was big, good-looking, and stupid." I remember her saying this in front of my two boys, which made me wince.

The first fictional father was the one who popped up when I searched with parameters like "Navy" and "1966" and "Connecticut." He retired from Pratt & Whitney and coached American Legion baseball in West Hartford. This guy could be a fit, I thought. The age group was correct; Pratt & Whitney supplied the military, and surely a guy would have to know about electrical systems to work at a huge company that makes turbine engines, right? American Legion meant he'd seen action in some war in some division of the military (for my purposes I assigned Vietnam and the Navy). He was from Connecticut, he was in the Navy (in my imagination), and if he'd coached baseball, I figured he might be big, good-looking, and stupid.

I copied his contact information off the American Legion coaching staff website, right down to his address, e-mail, home and cell phone numbers. Then came the hard part. How should I contact him in a way that would elicit a response, any response?

I began futzing around with the concept of writing a letter to my would-be father. I decided it would have to be an old-fashioned letter, one on real stationery, written in ink. It seemed to be that this style of letter might be harder for him to refute. I worried he wouldn't be able to read my tragic handwriting, and then I feared he would connect my handwriting to Ursula's, which was also sprawling and hard to read. In deciding to begin a search for my birth father, that search would have to start with a letter that began with a salutation and ended with *sincerely*. After I mailed it I would have to sit back and wait for a reply.

> Hi Mr. Sanford,
> I am doing some fact checking for a client of mine who is writing a book. I am an editor and proofreader, and you can see my qualifications online at my website . . .

No, that didn't work. The salutation was too familiar in tone, and it begins with a lie since I was pretending to be my own client. No one should start a relationship with a lie.

> Dear Mr. Sanford,
> I found your name in an Internet search and am wondering if you wouldn't mind helping me with some genealogical research I'm conducting. I am interested in finding a Dick Sanford who was in the Navy in the late '60s in Florida. I'm putting together a family tree and am trying to fill in some missing pieces.
> The particular Dick Sanford I'm looking for grew up (or lived for a while) in Ridgefield, CT, went to a technical school and was an electrician's mate in the Navy from 1966 onward.
> I would very much appreciate your help in filling in some information for me. I grew up in Redding, CT, and the Sanford family essentially founded the town there. You can imagine this is an essential genealogy of a prominent family who

founded Redding, CT. There has been quite a lot of research done already, it seems.

I won't take up much of your time, but I would like to understand if I'm on the right track here. I would appreciate a response even if you are not the correct person. If you're able to suggest further leads, that would be helpful.

Feel free to email me anytime. Thank you so much,

Megan

The query was plausible, placid, and real if you don't count the sin of omission that I might be his daughter. I wasn't lying. I wasn't curving the truth. I was carving the truth. I had a poker face in this email, I was not revealing my real motivations, and I was not threatening or asking for anything. What was the point of that anyway? The message above was a whole lot better than this one, which certainly sets a tone.

Dear Mr. Sanford,

Remember back in May or June of 1966? You were dating a woman named Ursula before you went into the Navy in Florida? Remember her? She got pregnant. You remember, I bet. It may not be a happy memory for you, but I've had a happy life. I have every indication that you may be my biological father and I would really love to meet you. I've met her.

I'm not looking for an extended relationship (unless you want that) or to upset your life or your family in any way. They don't ever have to know about me if you don't want them to (although I don't see the shame in it). I want to meet you and talk with you and see if we resemble each other because that's important to me. I have two boys, almost grown teenagers, and I bet they look like you. I feel like it would put me at ease to know my birth father and to see a resemblance in your face. I've been trying to write about this experience and have started work on a collection of essays, and I figure the least I can do is offer you the opportunity to have a voice. Ursula has her voice, and I'm trying to figure out where I fit in the grand scheme of the story as she tells it. I'd really like to hear your version of events to understand you better so I can understand myself better. That's all that really matters to me, although if you volunteered to pay for my MFA, I'd surely let you (that was a joke, okay a half-serious joke).

Sincerely yours,
Megan

The last and the most promising candidate is the guy who owns Richard Sanford Electric in Norwalk, Connecticut. It would make sense that, as an electrician's mate in the Navy, you might come home to start a business in electrical contracting. What would be insanely weird about this scenario is that we had likely met. Sanford Electric was a place where my dad (a contractor after his stint as a high school English teacher) would have stopped to get supplies while we were on the way to my grandparents' beach house in Rowayton, Connecticut. I remember spending a lot of time in such places, pawing through plastic junction boxes and miscellaneous parts. I especially loved the lighting stores where I could cavort around, flicking chandeliers on and off and pressing the display doorbells wired for sound.

Contacting this Dick Sanford might require a simple phone call, but what to say?

"Hi, is Richard there?"

"Richard Sanford?"

"Yes."

"Senior or junior?"

"The father, please."

"He's retired. May I ask who is calling?"

"Oh, it's the daughter of a friend he knew back before he went into the Navy. I was just trying to get in touch with him."

This was the part where the guy would tell me that this particular Dick Sanford was either in the Navy or was not. If he answered yes, I would ask, "Is there a way that's best to reach him?"

———

The impact of a father on a girl's life is a profound and well documented. If the relationship was based on emotional or physical abuse or was non-existent to begin with, people will accuse a girl of having "daddy issues." The term applies as a basic and derogatory catchall about women who try to claim their sexuality. Girls with daddy issues, according to the male fantasy, are easy conquests. It is also a classic double bind and a version of the Madonna-Whore complex.

There's a saying: "Absent fathers make nuts and sluts."

I was a college girl who traded sex on the hopeful idea that I wasn't a one-night stand. I faked orgasms. I lost my virginity at nineteen in a furtive fuck with my first real boyfriend. Ironically, he was in the Navy and, well, stupid. He came just as I was beginning to enjoy it and lived at home with his parents. I let him fuck me doggy style in his childhood bed; give me what he called a "nose job" through my jeans in his parents' bedroom; and I didn't object when he suggested I wear his mother's nurses uniform for Halloween so he could sneak me into a bar with him because I was underage. Was I "easy"? Was I a "slut"?

I'm furious at the double standard and systemic misogyny leveled at women who surrender their children, but not at fathers who outright abandon the women they've impregnated.

Why had I not felt the same fervor to know my biological father as I did my birth mother? Why was I getting serious about searching for him at a time when he could most likely be dead? I typed "Dick Sanford Obituary," and the search returned this:

Richard A. "Dick" Sanford Sr., 72, died Friday, Feb. 7, 2014, at his home in Ledyard, surrounded by his loving family and cat named Munchkin after his courageous battle with cancer.

Dick was born June 13, 1941, in Lockport, N.Y., the son of Charles Sanford and Mable (Robinson) Sanford. He honorably served in the U.S. Navy for 22 years until his retirement in 1990. Afterwards, he worked in the maintenance department at Waterford Country School.

Dick was predeceased by his wife of 45 years, Charlotte (Grant) Sanford, two brothers, and a sister.

The time frame fits. The extent of his service in the Navy matches. He lived in New London, Connecticut, and died there.

Was he my father? I'll never know, because I can't write a letter to my dead dad and expect a reply.

Daddy, 1966.
Courtesy Michael B. Culhane.

You could play by yourself in your playpen for hours

The Girl, the Garden, and the Key

There once was a young woman who lived in cages of her own making. Her name was False Self. The cages were beautiful. She'd built them with First Prince and they'd loved each other for a long and happy time.

The cages felt safe for a while, but as she grew and changed, she despaired at how she'd locked her True Self away. She'd put her heart under glass behind a walled garden deep inside herself. She'd go there sometimes to look at her heart and feel free. The door to the garden could have easily been opened with a key, but she kept the key hidden so well that even she couldn't find it.

———

False Self met First Prince through Best Friend, but First Prince had a daughter and was going through a divorce. He also lived three hours from her at the time, so False Self was like "meh, whatever."

Best Friend saw the raw, real parts of False Self, the silly let's-wear-clay-face-masks-eat-Doritos-and-watch-*Beverly-Hills-90210* side, and the serious let's-talk-into-the-night-about-our-past side. They worked together at

189

Cornell. Best Friend witnessed the beginnings of True Self.

False Self dated a bunch of men at Cornell. She didn't have a type. She had no idea who she was or what she wanted, she just wanted men and she wanted men to want her. There was José the clothing designer, Scott the soccer player, and Scott the athletic trainer. There was that guy the psychic said she'd have a relationship with before he went to Japan, there was the guy who was staying on a friend's couch on his trip through town, there was Dale the campus security guard. She'd had a crush on both Tim and Pete, her two best friends. She *really* loved Patrick the smart, sensitive lacrosse player. She went to therapy because she'd begun throwing up again trying to fit herself into all the boxes she tried to put herself in. She performed sex instead of enjoying it. She hadn't realized she should have been pleasing herself first.

Desire is a motherfucker.

False Self convinced herself she'd never marry: not because she chose independence (she hadn't thought that to even *be* a choice then) but because she felt unworthy of anyone's love.

First Mother—the adopted mother she considered to be her "first"—reminded her that "marriage is hard work."

She'd never been sold a Cinderella story.

———

First Prince was the first man who declared his love for her. He was handsome and kind and comfortable as a slipper.

False Self hadn't acknowledged her fears. Her body wasn't feeling pleasure with First Prince, but instead of seeing a red flag, she set about trying to be the thing that would give him pleasure.

She began receiving subtle messages about the cage she was willingly locking herself inside. For her wedding, First Mother gave her a sheer white, cotton Lanz of Salzburg nightgown that seemed virginal.

When False Self had First Son, Only Father draped her head in a white blanket and made her pose for photos as though she was the Madonna with Child. She and First Prince talked about wanting to have children, but now he wanted them sooner rather than later because he *didn't want to have gray hair when the kids were in kindergarten.*

She felt both young and old; as if marriage and children were to be had before the age of thirty on some prescribed societal timeline. As if she didn't hit the proper marks she'd be rendered a crone forever.

Be the Madonna, not the Whore read all the messages. But both were inside her in equal measure.

———

When False Self was a child, her favorite books were *The Lonely Doll, The Velveteen Rabbit, Corduroy,* and *Thumbelina.*

All the books were about characters—dolls, bears, rabbits, a miniature orphan—wishing themselves into existence, hoping love would make them real, and feel held, and hugged. Adult True Self was amazed it took her so long to see her self, given how much information had been right in front of her eyes.

She had been a solitary child. She'd created worlds into which she could disappear for hours, but unlike *Alice's Adventures in Wonderland* or Sarah in *Labyrinth,* she hadn't realized she held the key to her own happiness. She'd assigned other people the power over that.

False Self had recurring nightmares as a child. A towering black Louise Bourgeois-like spider chased her in circles around the lawn of her girlhood home. She was barefoot and running. She could hear the snap of the spider's pincer mandibles—big as the family car—and the thunder of each one of its eight legs as they dented the grass behind her.

"Turn and face that spider," said Only Father when she told him she was scared. "Yell at it to go away."

The next time the spider showed up in her dream she began to run, but stopped and turned on her bare heels in the damp dream grass. She balled up her fists, held them at her sides and screamed "Goooooo Awayyyyy" at the top of her lungs. The spider shattered like a mirror into tiny pieces that fell tinkling in a reflective pile on the grass. The dream never came again.

———

She thought First Prince had saved her. False Self wasn't exactly sure she needed to be saved, but at that time she feared being alone. She busied herself pleasing others— her bosses, her mother-in-law, her family, Only Father, First Prince, and society's expectations.

She was hiding bits of herself from him—her deepest thoughts and desires. She kept those in the secret walled garden inside herself. It was a place she'd go to be alone and she got upset when he tried to follow her there.

And yet, she clung to First Prince like he was one of Harry Harlow's wire monkeys. It was neither fair to him, nor satisfying to her, but she equated being alone with being abandoned.

After many years she realized she'd abandoned herself.

———

She and First Prince lived in three splendid and very different castles, the last one was of their own making and included a barn for the horses she raised and trained, and for the cows, pigs, goats, and chickens First and Second Son raised to eat.

First Castle was a gigantic farmhouse with a widow's peak. They lived there in the months before they were married. It was full of mice, haunted by a matriarch of a ghost, and fell under the haunted gaze of its twin built on the wooded hill up the road. Once, its yard was cut through by a tornado that took down the barn's wooden silo.

There, she read Amy Bloom's story "Silver Water," and identified with Rose running out into the backyard at night, barefoot, the jar of Seconal in her fist: The moon carrying her up and up toward salvation.

———

First Son was the apple of her eye and yet after he was born she dreamed terrifying scenarios in which she crashed through a causeway guardrail to avoid an oncoming truck and plunged into a reservoir—down and down and down and down. False Self saved herself but couldn't free First Son from his car seat. She surfaced to breathe, but when she dove back down, the car had plunged so deep she couldn't reach him.

Her therapist told her to imagine a stop sign when she has these thoughts. She told her to yell STOP! out loud. False Self tried this, but also avoided the causeway altogether, choosing to drive ten miles out of the way to keep First Son safe from her own mind.

Second Son was born and he was the ultimate snuggler; the one who held her face with his tiny hands so he could look into her eyes as if to say "there you are." At night she'd find him with his head facing the footboard, or kneeling on the floor, his torso bent over the bed, mouth open and drooling. She'd reposition him, his eyes would open a squinch and he'd smile up at her all sleep drunk. She was deeply in love.

They'd brought him home to Second Castle—a wee 900-square foot cottage in a tiny Upstate New York village—that they'd renovated from top to bottom in a frugal, cheerful way.

First Son's bedroom had six layers of wallpaper to steam off. She stripped away the previous owner's lives back to the '40s, while imagining her future. In his room she hung The Cow Jumped Over the Moon wallpaper. Second Son's bedroom was so small (a former closet) it barely fit his toddler bed. They found a taxidermy pheasant in the crawl space above. The toilet was under an eve and her sons bathed together in the claw foot tub, ran naked in the backyard, and peed on trees.

After years of searching, she found Birth Mother and talked with her on the telephone for the first time, lying on her bed like a teenager.

False Self could make a paperboard box feel like home; First Prince was a skilled craftsman who could fix anything.

After the divorce, Second Son pushed her away the hardest and didn't talk to her for a very, very long time.

———

False Self and First Prince had considered day care but the expense was so great they decided one of them would stay home. First Prince worried he wouldn't be able to find a job with just an associate's degree. Being an at-home dad would allow him time to *figure out what he wanted to do when he grew up*, he said. So, armed with her journalism degree, False Self set out to secure a job that led to bigger and more high-powered jobs.

She became Breadwinner.

First Prince was an excellent at-home dad. He made homemade pies and False Self accused him of trying to show her up. He saw the boys through chicken pox, lice infestations, and appendix scares among other things. They'd run to him when they were hurt and that hurt False Self's feelings most of all because it meant she was a bad mother and failing at trying to "do it all."

Once, in what was supposed to be a quiet moment, she rocked in the hammock nursing Second Son. First Son emerged from around a tree with dog feces smeared all over his hands. In her haste to get up, she placed Second Son too close to the edge of a hammock; he fell out and thumped his tiny forehead on the tree root sticking out of the dirt below. Everyone screamed. A lump the size of a hard-boiled egg grew on his forehead. She felt like a terrible mother.

False Self made work friends and occasionally wanted to go out and have fun—just the girls. This was hard on First Prince, who didn't understand why False Self would need anyone other than him. She'd cry. She had no family here, she said. Family surrounded him. He chalked it up to her being hormonal, so she stopped asking to go out and instead threw herself into caring for her family, otherwise she'd have been Bad Wife *and* Bad Mother.

She visited her walled garden more frequently.

Where'd you go? he'd ask.

————

First Prince stayed home with the boys for ten years. Together they built Third Castle. He decided that what he wanted to do when he grew up was custom woodworking so they created a woodshop in the basement of Third Castle and Only Father—also a woodworker—gave him many of his tools. First Prince designed and made a dinner table from salvaged wood. Everyone who sat around it wanted to buy the table. False Self encouraged him; she was in marketing, she could make his website and find clients. She gave him time to do his projects at night and on the weekends, and he'd putter down in his shop. He said he worried that turning his hobby into a business would ruin his love of doing it and that's when she realized he was content to stay un-grown-up.

First Prince worked for cash under-the-table for two millionaires. *Twenty-five dollars an hour without taxes is the equivalent of $35 or $40 an hour if I were paying taxes,* he'd say when she suggested he form his own contracting business. It nagged at her that she never knew how much he really made and she wondered if he was hiding something else like he was hiding the thousands in cash she found in the front pocket of a shirt hanging in the closet.

I use that to pay the property taxes, he said.

She worried she'd one day awaken to find news of another family he was supporting in a different state.

You're paranoid, he'd say. *It's always been just you.*

She'd forget to write the debits in the checkbook, which led to unaccounted-for expenses at the end of the month. He'd get annoyed about the lunches she was having with her work friends. *That $20 a day here and there adds up,* he'd say.

Let's make a budget, said False Self. *It would make me feel comfortable knowing exactly what I can spend on lunches or groceries.*

We just need to spend less than we make, it's that simple, he said.

She was making more than $100,000.

Maybe you should leave the debit card at home, First Prince said.

So she cut herself off from her own money supply. If she needed cash she'd have to ask him for it. From then on, First and Second Son saw her hold out her hand and ask for gas money or lunch money or any spending money. He'd sometimes say, *This is my last $20,* or, *Are you going to lunch again?* when he opened his wallet.

———

I'm tweaked that you're using Dad's money to get an apartment, said First Son when, years later, she told him she was moving out.

She felt stabbed in her heart garden. *Why do you think it's Dad's money?* she asked.

Because you're always asking him for money, said First Son. So she sat him down and told him the tale of how she'd been Breadwinner all these years.

Now she saw how they saw her: They didn't see her at all. She'd let that happen.

She'd created a home where everyone else's feelings were accounted for but hers didn't matter. She'd neglected to show her feelings and perhaps that meant they thought she didn't have any. In the end, that didn't feel much like home.

When she confided in Birth Mother that she was thinking of getting a divorce, she said *but he took care of you, and let you work all those high-powered jobs by staying home with the kids.*

As they were building Third Castle, First Mother died of pancreatic cancer. False Self held her hand when she died and Only Father cried in the chair next to her hospice bed in their bedroom. Only Father was gripped by grief in the years that followed. False Self made panicked calls to his neighbors: *Can you see his light on? Can you please check on him to make sure he's not collapsed on the floor? He's not answering his phone.*

False Self assumed the mantle as Everyone's Mother. She opened her home, which was decorated in the style of First Mother and Only Father. She welcomed everyone. She tried to recreate the magical Christmases and birthdays of their childhood until she collapsed under the Martha Stewart weight of it all. She'd thought it was what she'd wanted to do, and in part it was, but really she hadn't yet found the words to ask for support nor had she felt worthy enough to accept help.

She couldn't remember where she'd hid her key anymore. For a long time she forgot about her secret garden altogether.

One afternoon, Second Son came to stand in front of False Self who had been lying in bed all day with her sadness.

Come on, Mom, play with me, he'd said grabbing her hand. She felt a tear slip down her face. *I'm not feeling very well, sweetie,* she'd said.

Please Mom?

While they were throwing the ball back and forth, he asked, *Mom, am I the reason you're so sad?* and it broke open her heart.

———

After First Mother died, Only Father had many crises and False Self rushed to help.

First and Second Son had their share of crises as well: ruptured appendix, brushes with the police, hunting violations, pot smoking, school suspension, ADD diagnosis, and major knee surgery, to name a few.

Her boys called her "Mama Bear." She was proactive: hiring lawyers, researching consequences, finding therapists, fretting about "what-ifs." First Prince was laissez-faire: *Things will get better,* he'd say, or *It'll work itself out,* as if magic was supposed to fix things. As if inaction was action.

Why do you avoid conflict? she said.

Why do you run to it? he said.

They were living in their final Castle—the one they'd built together in the hayfield dotted now with an overgrown riding ring, rusty farm equipment, the hulks of old trucks, and half-finished projects. She'd placed the key to her walled garden in the cement when they'd poured the foundation because she thought surely this was to be her final Castle.

She planted her dead mother's daylilies around the foundation. She began making To-Do lists—a calendar of weekends and chores so they could finish unfinished projects together because, surely then, he could begin the woodworking he wanted to do when he grew up. Instead, he'd dodge, weave, distract, and putter. She'd seethe, resent, demand, and withdraw. It was emotional épée.

First Prince became reticent and complacent. She tried to let go of control. Over time, they transitioned from Good Cop/Bad Cop to Martyr/Nag.

No one wants to be married to a doormat, said False Self's friends.

She went to therapy again and discovered what codependency and passive aggression meant. She watched with wider eyes as Birth Mother and In-Laws enacted both as if it were a Shakespearian tragedy.

I worry we're turning into them, she said to First Prince.

———

Her body broke first—it always did—and False Self ignored every warning sign because she'd convinced herself she was *stronger than that.* Every new and bigger job she took came with a different and more serious health crisis: depression, near-fatal ectopic pregnancy, thoughts of suicide, and a nervous breakdown. While her body kept its dark score, she was medicated and self-medicated.

She'd almost bled to death from the ectopic pregnancy seven years after Second Son was born. Coming out of the anesthesia, False Self remembered thinking, *I nearly died: Is this the man I want to be with for the rest of my life?* It was the first clear voice of True Self, but she couldn't yet hear it.

After she'd almost died, so did their sex life. At first she'd thought her lack of interest was because she was afraid of dying from another tubal pregnancy.

She'd become dry as a desert. She recoiled when First Prince touched her. Instead of seeing these as symptoms of her feelings for him, she became convinced she was in full menopause. She became the confirmed patient in the marriage.

I thought we were just in the woods, said First Prince who didn't know what menopause was. *I thought we'd eventually come out of the woods.*

Once you're in the woods, there's no coming out, she said.

She asked First Prince to get a vasectomy and he balked. *This isn't about you,* she said.

True Self's voice was waking up slowly by shutting her body down piece by piece. *Listen to me,* the voice said. *Hear me out.* But her mind seemed intent on self-oblivion and her heart was now locked up tight in the garden.

In this way False Self erased herself, and she'd fooled First Prince which wasn't fair. She'd never given herself a chance to fall in love with herself. He'd fallen in love with someone who hadn't existed.

———

False Self was excellent at hiding in plain sight. She excelled at her jobs as the voice of college presidents and chancellors, spending years mastering and mirroring their speech patterns so she could write convincingly in their voice so they could gain prestige, raise more money, and be the experts in their field.

Long ago, while performing tests with her violin to get into college, a man plunking notes on the piano told her she had perfect pitch. First Mother used to say she wanted everything to be perfect.

She'd thought she liked the word *perfect*, but *perfect* had become the spider from her childhood dreams.

She'd been laid off, left, and was fired from her last three jobs where her bosses had been indicted for state ethics panel violations; driven out by the trustees; and left due to incompetence and for having an affair with the college president.

She felt like she was coming apart at the wheels, like the walls around her garden were being smashed and broken by something trying to get at her. She Googled, "What is a Nervous Breakdown?" She went to see a new Pill Popping Therapist because she felt her mind was defying her.

Have you had thoughts of suicide? Pill Popping Therapist asked.

False Self was afraid to share her real feelings. She said she didn't want to be institutionalized. She had children. She was The Breadwinner. She made Pill Popping Therapist promise she wouldn't send her away to the Looney Bin.

I've been thinking lately how easy it would be to get up to 100 mph and slam my car straight into a tree, she said.

Well, that's very specific, said Pill Popping Therapist.

The only problem is that I bought this stupidly expensive Volvo station wagon and it's one of the safest cars on the road so I'd likely walk away with barely a scratch, she said through tears. *See? I'd even fail at committing suicide.*

I feel like I'm worth more to my family dead than alive, she said. *At least they can collect the insurance when I'm gone.*

Pill Popping Therapist gave her Clonazepam and suggested she get the hell out of the job with Headmistress.

Cut one in half ten minutes before your meetings, she said.

She worked up the nerve to demand Headmistress pay her out of her contract. *This is obviously not working for you and it's obviously not working for me,* said False Self.

Look at you, modeling bravery, said Headmistress.

She gave two weeks' notice and saved the Clonazepam in a small leather pouch stashed in her bedside table. She has them still, all these years later.

———

Headmistress announced at the big meeting that False Self would be leaving so she could write her book. False Self wasn't working on a book. Headmistress made a big deal of giving her a Moleskin notebook and a pen in front of the leadership team. In truth, writing was the only thing False Self had ever wanted to do, but Nervous Breakdown had affected everyone in the family, including her beloved horses who stood knee deep in their own shit.

She got into a summer writing program. There she met a gentle, kind, teacher and another who would become a dear friend. Go to graduate school for writing, they both said. So she applied, not knowing what she didn't know.

Congratulations, that's nice, honey, Only Father said, when she told him of her acceptance.

First Prince gave her a laptop for Christmas. He bought her a sweatshirt from the school. He said, *We'll make it work,* when she worried about the cost of tuition because she was unemployed.

False Self met Her People in grad school. She no longer felt invisible.

You can't hide in your work, said one of her teachers. *Your faults as a person are your faults on the page.*

Everyone at school brought their wounds and piled them on the table in front of each other. *Here is my mess,* they'd say. *Help me make it better.*

She talked to her school friends about leaving First Prince. Her True Self was waking up.

I feel I can be my Whole Self here, she said.

After the nervous breakdown, True Self's first words to First Prince were, *I'm a failure.*

I can't do this anymore. I feel so alone.

————

True Self was at an artist residency in Virginia one February, which had been the month First Mother died almost fifteen years ago. The loss still felt fresh: the grief strong. She wrote poems about the full moon, and her rage at the boxes women are put in or put themselves in. She wrote about dead mothers and dead babies that had been discovered in a septic tank in Ireland. She flirted with an Irish composer and the handsome poet who stuttered and chose exactly the right words. Her body reawakened. She became wet with desire for a writer she traded work with but had never met. She didn't call home.

How's things at writer camp? First Prince said, calling her to check in.

I don't want to come home, she said, and he thought it was because of the Nor'easter blowing in.

Driving home into the storm, she stopped halfway at a hotel where she sat in her underwear and ordered ribs from room service as though it were her last meal.

Ever since you've been home it feels like you think this is jail, he said.

She asked for space. She moved upstairs to live in First Son's room and slept there for three months. First Prince did not come upstairs.

————

True Self moved into her own apartment after First Son's August wedding which was on the same day as First

Mother's birthday. She stood at the apartment door and stared at the key in her palm. She called the apartment her Sanctuary. It was above an independent bookstore. She bought herself a cozy chair from Craigslist and put it in the window, sunning herself like a cat. There she read and sipped hot coffee until noon.

She felt at peace. She loved the smell of the wood floors, and the sight of her lone toothbrush in the holder. She took baths, she talked for hours with friends on the phone, she cried with grief over leaving her husband, she tried to date, she had tea with her 85-year-old neighbor; she embraced the difference between being lonely and being alone. She leaned into herself.

Sitting on her couch, she replayed other people's narratives in her head as if they were a mixtape.

Did you try hard enough? said Only Father.

*No one will ever love you like First Prince loved y*ou, said Birth Mother.

———

The hardest breakups are the ones in which no one has done anything wrong. There was no cheating, or abuse, or secret gambling problem: Just a long, slow, decay.

———

Before she recognized the pattern, she had a long and tiresome love affair with unavailability. Married and avoidant men found her curious and beautiful and she reveled in their just-out-of- reach attention before realizing that the unrequited love stories were simply re-enacting the same pattern of abandonment that seemed most comfortable to her. She kept voting against her own self-interest. The person she was abandoning was herself.

She became less fearful there would be a Second Prince. She found a beautiful new castle to live in in a walkable city where she'd dwelled as a single girl nearly thirty years earlier. She felt she'd returned home.

She was determined to live openly from a place of tenderness and vulnerability. She required reciprocity from those she held dear, letting go of those who didn't rise to meet her.

No Prince would again have power over her because she wouldn't give them power.

Perhaps because it was June and because she was reading Anne Sexton she didn't want to be brave anymore.

Her new castle came with a key to a private park across the street. She went there often to sit in the sun or to watch the stars.

And she existed happily ever after.

You could play by yourself in your playpen
for hours. Courtesy of Michael B. Culhane.

Ursula as Ms. CN Tower, Toronto

Where There Is Nothing Left to Hide, There Is Nothing Left to Seek

On its face, an erotic watch looks much like any other pocket watch, but hidden between the dust cover and the inner gears is a secret door.

Open it.

Lascivious scenes range from static, full-color enameled couplings to a single nude female in a black and white photo hidden behind gilded covers. Each piece of important anatomy is rendered in precious metal, sometimes with moving parts on the dial. These are called automatons.

One watch depicts ménage a trois. A pair of Rubenesque women are fashioned in 14-carat gold against a gunmetal background; one stands with her legs splayed, the other is supine on her back on an ottoman with her face firmly planted in the other's fanny. Her right arm drapes toward the floor in ecstasy. The man is rendered in a darker metal, as if in shadow. He is kneeling on a pillowed footstool holding the supine woman's abundant thighs in the crook of his arms. He is bent at the shoulders, his head bowed in ecstasy. His hips pivot as the watch tics away the seconds—tic, tic, tic—forcing his tiny metal cock in and out like a metronome.

———

One of the first gifts Ursula gave me was a rose gold watch fob that had a Victorian mourning locket suspended on one end. Inside were blond strands of hair from a boy she called "Junior." Junior was "the other adoptee in the family," adopted within the family to conceal a relative's illegitimate birth.

I became obsessed with discovering everything I could about Junior and his adoptive parents. I speculated as to what type of pocket watch might have accompanied the ornate fob of a relative by marriage who was a wealthy nineteenth-century industrialist. Robert Gair invented the paperboard box and built the iconic Clock Tower building that hulks over what is now DUMBO Brooklyn. While researching timepieces, I discovered erotic automaton pocket watches.

Horology, the study of time and timepieces, is a phonetically lusty word—but erotic horology? Well, now that pricked my interest.

———

When Ursula told me the stories of her at 15-years-old "carrying on" with the young Army officers in Germany, I thought of her as daring and brave. But her family, society, and history judge independent-minded young women as threatening and promiscuous. Sex, in the end, is about power. Our bodies are paradox and myth: our lives a duality of Madonna *or* whore, never and.

"We have been taught to suspect this resource, vilified, abused, and devalued within western society," writes Audre Lorde in *Uses of the Erotic: The Erotic as Power*. "On the other hand, the superficially erotic has been encouraged as a sign of female inferiority; on the other hand, women have been made to suffer and to feel both contemptible and suspect by virtue of its existence."

———

I think of the story of Persephone and Demeter and how it persists, like the seasons, to arouse feelings about mother/daughter duality, rape, power, abandonment, and resilience. Persephone was abducted and raped by Hades. Her mother, Demeter—goddess of the seasons, abundant harvest, and the cycle of life—lost in grief and loneliness while searching for her, descended from the heavens and wandered the earth. There, she stopped time; halted the growth of all the living things. She rendered the land barren. She threatened humanity with extinction in the name of finding her daughter.

Is this where the phrase "I would go to the ends of the earth for you" comes from?

Demeter raged. She cried. She had a lot of big feelings. She was comforted by an earthly mother. She manufactured a winter of discontent. She covered the world in a blanket of famine until her brother/husband Zeus—who had brokered Persephone's abduction by Hades in the first place—intervened.

Who do you think was celebrated for saving the earth and who for destroying it?

Do you see how a narrative gets twisted?

Do you see how a God anoints himself hero to mankind simply by fixing his own fuck-up?

Because she ate one pomegranate seed, Persephone was tricked into sharing time with Hades for one-third of the year.

Women earn one-third less than men and likely will forevermore.

As a child who did not yet understand the allegory (but perhaps embodied the feeling), I composed my first piece of music by flashlight in the dark of my bedroom closet. I titled it "Persephone" and remember writing it to sound like a funeral dirge, as if I were drowning (which I was then, alone with my feelings and nowhere yet to put them).

I'd not yet tasted a pomegranate. I'd not yet been paid one-third less. I'd not yet understood why I'd felt the need to hide in my closet. I simply followed my feelings down a deep, dark hole and hid there for a long time—a late bloomer.

Secrets are the seeds of a good story.

An allegory is a concealed story.

———

Instead of channeling her independent streak, Ursula's parents concealed her. They sent her away to a convent school in Limerick, Ireland, run by The Salesian Sisters. Perhaps they thought they were protecting her. Perhaps they wanted to avoid their own shame at the complications between her desire and the consequences of it. Perhaps they thought time would change her.

When she later told me stories of her experiences there, she talked of the loneliness, deprivation, and punishments for rule-breaking behavior that to me sounded like normal teenage rebelliousness. She'd suffered severe chilblains—painful swelling of the small blood vessels in her skin especially her hands—from being made to take repeated cold baths in dirty water. All the girls shared one bathtub and as punishment, the nuns made Ursula take her bath last. Then the nuns sent her to her room, dripping wet and without a towel. It was one of the many abandonments I feel she'd suffered.

The nuns withheld family letters and small comforts of snacks, and trinkets her family had mailed to her. These objects were not returned to her until she'd graduated early with straight A's. She'd applied and was accepted to prestigious women's colleges—Bennington, Wellesley, and Sarah Lawrence—but her parents made her again live under the watchful eyes of the church. They sent her away to Ladycliff College, a small Catholic school located at the base of West Point and run by the Franciscan Sisters. She was kicked out for drinking, smoking, staying out after curfew and cavorting with the Cadets.

A year later, she'd be pregnant with me.

———

Some of the earliest known examples of erotic pocket watches date back to seventeenth century China where luxury timepieces were created for the Emperor. King Louis XV of France popularized the timepieces among the aristocracy in the 1700s. Abraham Louis Bréguet, who was the watchmaker to Louis XVI and Marie-Antoinette, kept up the tradition through the 1800s with delicately wrought gold and silver figures featuring intricate moving parts. When daguerreotypes came into vogue, nude female photos were set under glass inside hidden cutout windows in the watches, giving an added air of titillating secrecy. In this way, women's bodies were constantly being looked at instead of seen. Held in a man's palm: concealed in a vest pocket.

Then there were ornate watches that must have been created for a filthy aristocracy. One of my favorites is rendered in 18-carat gold and blue enamel depicting an "animated coupling at 6 p.m." I admire its cheeky humor and that it seems to have been made for a couple in love.

Two figures depicted as a god and goddess stand on either side of the watch face holding mallets and ready to strike the noon or midnight hour together. We can see the inner workings of the watch "skeletonized" underneath the watch face. Below, at 6 p.m., are two miniature golden humans. The woman is on her back on a settee with her dress pushed above her waist. Her paramour is on top. Her legs are wrapped around her lover's hips. He is bent over her in his topcoat and tails, kneeling with his pants at his ankles. His large endowment is animated by the watch—in, out, in, out—as it counts the seconds. A chubby golden Cupid peeks out the right corner, naked and pointing at the couple as if to say, "get it."

The watch is described as having "cylindrical pillars, fuse and chain, verge escapement, and continental cock with a polished steel end piece."

Among other things, the sheer eroticism of the language turns me on.

"Outside the Abbey Walls," circa 1910, is an enameled tableau of a taboo tryst between a pair of un-humanly endowed Capuchin Friars in full robe "enjoying local hospitality in the woods." The friars have pulled their brown robes above their waists and their brightly colored pants down to their knees.

Their penises are depicted out of scale with mushroom tips, pink from friction, and curved upward in cocky smiles. The first Friar is plunged inside the prone "local" woman whose blue dress is pushed above her waist. Her right breast is flushed pink and exposed and one monk is bending to kiss it. She is splayed against a rock. The second monk, bearded in his hood, is taking full measure of the first Friar's behind.

―――――

Interest in erotic pocket watches, and erotic wristwatches has never waned especially among ardent collectors (mostly men.) The watches were made for men, by men. A man chose the scene, established the shot, and commissioned a specifically rendered portrait designed solely for his pleasure. Because these watches were customized to depict a specific erotic male fantasy, the women became both the subject and object of his desire.

I've read that men gave these watches to their mistresses, and gifted them to countries as talismans that cemented diplomatic trade agreements—this practice seems reminiscent of trading women like chattel. Today, this horological erotica can sell for six figures at auction houses like Antiquorum, in Geneva, Switzerland, that specialize in the timepieces. A small, secretive market thrives for these erotic watches and collectors include Elton John, among others.

―――――

Be it the seventeenth or the twenty-first century, the way we wear our technology is also the way we consume and conceal our desires. Erotic pocket watches were the pocket porn of the Early Modern Period just as the iPhone functions in a similar way today. Time hasn't changed the way we carry our secret fantasies, just the devices we use to deliver them to us.

Secrecy was a vital part of the erotic nature of a pocket watch, as it is for the erotic wristwatch. Concealment is fundamental to the heightening of desire. In her book *Mating in Captivity: Unlocking Erotic Intelligence,* author and psychotherapist Esther Perel writes, "Where there is nothing left to hide, there is nothing left to seek."

———

The women who ran the orphan asylums and foundling homes of the nineteenth century viewed themselves as evangelical reformers of "fallen women." They believed it was sinful women who were responsible for illegitimate births—men played no part in this narrative and were free to enjoy sex with whomever they desired with no negative consequences. Women who found themselves pregnant had little choice but to have the baby and leave it to be found in a public park, on a street, or in an alley (hence the term "foundling"), or try to raise it themselves despite a society poisoned by the notion of single motherhood.

". . . By relieving women of the products of their sin and keeping their secrets, foundling asylums could rescue fallen women from what they saw as an inevitable downward spiral into prostitution," wrote Julie Miller in her book *Abandoned*.

Time hasn't changed how society views women and babies born out of wedlock. Secrecy and concealment were vital to the paradox of protecting babies, and demonizing mothers. Shame, the byproduct, kept women quiet.

———

A mark of social status and wealth, pocket watches were the peacocks of timepieces: A way to display a man's power.

An erotic pocket watch was a specific commitment—a bespoke object of desire crafted by some of the finest Swiss watchmakers in the world like the Cortébert (which supplied parts to Rolex); Breguet et Fils, whose watches featured minutely detailed mechanically operated erotic scenes rendered in fine metals and enamel; and Doxa whose specialty was enameled, painted scenes that were lifelike, if not a bit cartoonish. A buyer had control over the specificity of every single aspect of the watchmaking, from the type of scene, to the many "complications," to the types of precious metals. The object had one or two specific functions back then: to tell the date and the time. Because of its specificity it was an intimate object with a deliberate, focused intent.

I'm interested in the concept of time and desire and how devices connect us across time. Do our iPhones, with their mountains of data and access to an avalanche of porn deliver nothing more than superficial intimacy? Can technology truly lay the groundwork for a deeper connection? All the dating apps are peddling the added functionality and further intimacy of video dating during the COVID-19 pandemic. I'm just waiting for a sustained and intelligent text conversation.

Do the dings, chirps, and swooshes of our cell phones create Pavlovian anticipation, or do they simply prioritize immediacy over intimacy? Instead of the Jane Austen version of waiting days or weeks for a lover's thoughtful letter to arrive by foot or on horseback, do we now crave the immediacy of a phone call, FaceTime, or text? Computer-mediated intimacy seems decidedly less appealing than seeing a beloved's handwritten words on paper, or receiving the gift of a watch depicting an intimate and memorable coupling. Few people, when dating, write letters anymore (or even thoughtful emails). I'd like to bring that practice back. Instead it's all, "heyyy," "you up?" and "send nudes."

No one is standing in the rain outside my window holding a boombox over his head.

No one is broadcasting a guerilla radio show straight into my heart.

———

The erotic watch existed long before the photograph, and I argue they were pornographic rather than erotic because they typically depicted a graphic fetish or fantasy.

"Pornography ordinarily represents the sexual organs," wrote Roland Barthes in *Camera Lucida*, "making them into a motionless object (a fetish), flattened like an idol that does not leave its niche . . ."

Lacking an erotic complication there is nothing to drive a spark, nothing to deliver that twinge of desire that fuels my interest. Immediacy is a drain on yearning. Anticipation is the true longing.

I want my Lloyd Dobler. I want my Mark Hunter.

———

To know the time in the nineteenth century was a privilege. It was information not everyone had, unless you were wealthy enough to afford a timepiece. A pocket watch was considered a sign that the wearer (always a man) was reliable, punctual, and of good moral standing.

The four faces on Gair's Clock Tower still keep time over the East River.

Was Gair an egalitarian who wanted everyone to have the same information he did, or did he simply want his factory workers to be punctual?

———

The magic of a talisman lies in its story, doesn't it? I feel protected by and protective of this watch fob, this story, and this tenuous piece of my heritage. It contains a secret I can choose to share or conceal.

———

Pocket watches, like pockets themselves, are gendered objects. Wealthy nineteenth-century industrialists (all male) were upwardly mobile Captains of Industry, whereas women were relegated to their sphere of influence—the home. Men had pockets designed specifically for the purpose of carrying a pocket watch, among other things. Pockets in their trousers concealed wallets, keys, pocketknives, and business cards. Women's clothing of the nineteenth century didn't contain pockets, so many women wore diminutive wristwatches and ring watches, or timepieces on necklaces. It was considered scandalous at the time for women to show their ankles. As Chelsea G. Summers wrote in her article "The Politics of Pockets," concealment by women was a political threat:

"Women's pockets were private spaces they carried into the public with increasing freedom, and during a revolutionary time, this freedom was very, very frightening. The less women could carry, the less freedom they had. Take away pockets hidden in undergarments and you limit women's ability to navigate public spaces, to carry seditious (or merely amorous) writing, or to travel unaccompanied."

Victorian-era women were considered objects of desire, and consequently had to confine that desire to the marital bedroom or risk being labeled "loose" or "amoral." Victorians themselves were a paradox of unbridled lust and Puritanism, so the erotic pocket watch seemed the perfect object of sexual liberty and sexual secrecy.

I imagine Gair may have led many a board meeting, at which he checked his timepiece (erotic or not) a few times.

Ursula didn't begin to "show" until she was five months along with me. She said she kept waiting and waiting for her period to arrive. It didn't come of course, so she was again forced into concealment in the late '60s—this time with twenty other unwed mothers at The Guild of the Infant Saviour. Strict schedules, boredom, and the *TV Guide* metered out their days. "All we had was time," she said.

They'd been sent to hide their secret shame, and when it was over, they hoped to return to their normal lives as if no time had elapsed at all.

Erotic pocket watches remain highly collectible today, according to Mitch Greenblatt and his brother Andrew, who own watches.com and specialize in sourcing erotic timepieces.

One notable Swiss watchmaker, Svend Anderson of Andersen-Geneve, manufactures a bestselling line of custom erotic wristwatches called "Eros." All watches are by commission and nearly all his clientele is male. To date, his company has manufactured 171 of these custom erotic wristwatches. As you can imagine, the client list is a secret.

In his book *The Pleasure Principle,* Sigmund Freud argued that instincts fell into two categories—Eros (life giving, driven by the forces of pleasure and procreation) and Thanatos (the concept that "the goal of all life is death"). It's ironic then that the erotic watches that tick away hours of one's life are called Eros, which seems to reinforce the narrative of procreate or die.

———

True sexual intimacy is the most analog of experiences. Nothing can replace the feeling of a lover's body—skin to skin—or their heartbeat that is nearer and more constant than technological innovation could ever bring us.

The buzzed, flushed euphoria that comes from two human beings connecting in the most primal and non-technological way means eye contact, touch, smell, taste, and a heightening of all five senses: the very thing that the devices in our pockets threaten to deaden. Intimacy, therefore, is the exact opposite of concealment.

Wearing an object of desire so boldly on the wrist is certainly a provocative and titillating choice. These watches seem the antithesis of concealment. They are brazen and predatory public flauntings of male desire.

Erotic wristwatches today are made in limited quantities and coveted by collectors.

The Richard Mille RM69 Erotic Tourbillon, crafted of Grade 5 titanium, was released in 2015. It retailed for $750,000. It isn't pictorial, like its vintage counterparts, but rather imparts its mechanical seduction via words stacked on three rotating titanium bands:

"Let me kiss
you tonight;" and

"I want
to caress
you madly"; or

"I'd love to kiss
your pussy;" or

"I long to explore
your lips"

These watches were produced in a limited edition of thirty.

The power reserve lasts for sixty-nine hours.

According to advertisements, the "you" in the watch's message is meant to arouse desire in the observer, to pique her curiosity, draw her toward the wearer.

"Its name is a clear affirmation of the creative longing to reveal our most secret intentions in all their glory," says the advertising copy.

———

I never did get to the bottom of whether Gair owned an erotic pocket watch, but I cherish the watch fob and locket. Through the lens of time I've learned about generational ideas of sex, pleasure, and sin. Time may not change the way we consume our desire (or the way it consumes us), but does it change the way we conceal it?

Due to the social, moral, and political culture of the Victorian era, erotic pocket watches were banned, confiscated, or destroyed, making them even more valuable today.

Of the antique watches, the auction houses wrote descriptions of the parts of the watches, which seem erotically charged. Would-be buyers may understand these watch terms, but I don't know what they mean exactly. Instead, I find them titillating in their syntax. Descriptions include terms such as: "frilly hands," "gilt figures operated in unison," "continental cock with marquisate stones," and "not offending anyone with gentle sensibilities."

These watches were rarely commissioned for wives. They were made for lovers and "kept women," which meant a man could compartmentalize an affair and keep his lover neatly tucked away, physically and metaphorically—in his vest pocket—concealment being the exact reason for the thrill.

In essence, men of the time had women exactly where they wanted them, in their vest pocket.

Erotic timepieces convey desire in word and image, but always through the male gaze.

Every single watch I've researched has a nude woman at its secret center.

———

Ursula emailed me immediately after Dr. Blasey Ford's testimony in the Brett Kavanaugh Supreme Court hearings to convey her "déjà vu disgust." Time, it seems, hasn't changed this story where women's bodies are concerned. The Patriarchy views women as vessels that bear children, not as whole people. Time is a privilege still afforded to men. They can erase it, black out, move on, and be confirmed for life.

———

I'm left to question why it is that fully sexualized women offend "gentle sensibilities" in a way that must be hidden behind tiny golden doors? Did my ancestor carry an erotic pocket watch? I don't know. He was a shrewd Scotsman known for playing things close to the vest and, as a captain of industry, must have overseen many boring meetings.

And what of the women? Who is the woman who is attracted to the man wearing a Richard Mille Erotic Tourbillon?

According to watchmaker Andersen, the most difficult and important thing to achieve with an erotic automaton is that the couple moves "smoothly and in harmony."

This, I'd argue, is a timely metaphor for love and desire in all its forms.

Permission not granted

Do you still have your virginity, or just the box it came in?

Losing It

It was the summer of 1984, and all my friends were losing it. Senior year in high school was when they all lost their virginity. S lost it with her boyfriend on the floor in her parent's study while they were eating in the dining room; R lost it with Keith, who also hit her and left bruises; L lost it with her boyfriend who drove a garbage truck like her father.

I wouldn't be losing anything but my car keys for two more years.

I had just turned seventeen and was getting sick of hearing "I think I'm late," so one Saturday I packed them all into my robin's egg blue Chevy Chevette under pretenses of going to the mall, and drove them to Planned Parenthood in Danbury, Connecticut.

"If you're going to do it," I said, "at least don't get pregnant."

"The only way I'm getting fitted for a diaphragm is if you get one too," said R from the backseat.

———

I was making chocolate chip cookies after school when L's call jangled our mustard-colored rotary telephone.

She sounded upset but wouldn't tell me about what over the phone. I left the cookie dough and walked the half-mile to her house.

"Will you help me?" she asked after telling me she was pregnant. She'd already scheduled the appointment. I drove her into Danbury again that summer—this time for an abortion.

———

I remember the picketers holding signs. I don't remember what the signs said, just the protesters' red, angry faces pressed close to the car windows as we turned into the driveway. They shouted at us, their mouths contorted.

The waiting room at the clinic was decorated in a seventies color palette of browns and mustard. I sat on a Naugahyde chair and stared straight ahead for what seemed like hours. I half expected to hear a scream of pain, but mostly I had no idea what to expect.

When the nurse told me I could see L, she was sitting up in a chair, still in her hospital gown. She was in tears, rocking back and forth holding her abdomen.

"They made me look at it," she said.

———

R always left her diaphragm on the edge of the bathtub just to antagonize her mother.

"You have to put it in its case with cornstarch," I said, "or it will get holes in it. Was I the only one listening?"

S went on the Pill and did a lot of screwing around before meeting her husband. On her wedding day, he announced he had re-enlisted in the Navy. L went to the senior prom with her boyfriend, and they later married.

I didn't have one date in high school.

———

My feet were in the stirrups, and I scooched my butt down toward the end of the exam table as instructed. The tissue paper crinkled. I tried not to think about his eyes on me.

"So, tell me why you're here," said the doctor at Planned Parenthood. My friends were in adjoining exam rooms. The nurse stood behind him.

"I brought my friends because they need diaphragms," I said. "They told me they wouldn't get them unless I get fitted too."

"Have you had sex yet?" he asked.

I felt the cold metal of the speculum as he opened it fast and wide. I gasped. It hurt. I felt a warm trickle of blood.

"No," I said.

"Oh," he looked up at the nurse.

"Let me get you a towel, sweetie," she said.

Trick and Treat

Water

It was summer, 1985. My parents had dropped me off at Camp Lohikan in the Poconos. It was a typical sleep-away summer camp. Pristine Lake Como, dotted with the colorful sails of bobbing Minifish, lay nestled between mountains of mature pines. The winding wooded hill opposite the lake was marked with brown cabins, a mess hall, tennis courts, riding stables, and the A-framed camp director's office, which was the only place you could make a phone call from the rotary phone on the wall, or buy soda in a can.

I'd taken the job as a camp counselor that year after being recruited at a summer job fair at Penn State. I was a freshman trying for a summer with the Peace Corps (turns out they didn't want an orchestra nerd turned journalism major). Instead, I wound up teaching horseback riding to pre-teens.

I arrived that summer dressed in turquoise and pink Jams, the official shorts of the mid-'80s, an emerald green polo shirt with the collar flipped, and mid-calf L. L. Bean duck boots.

———

We counselors learned about each other at orientation. We sat cross-legged in a circle on the open grass outside the mess hall and went slowly clockwise, prodded by the camp director, sharing a little bit about ourselves. There was a heavy-set guy studying to be a mortician; a wiry, pimply kid who liked skateboarding and comic books and who took to following me around; my friend Richie who was like everyone's brother; Belinda, an education major from Elmira College; Lesley, a troubled college dropout and fellow riding instructor; and Mike and Barb, who would become a couple that summer. Then there was Charlie, who kept me guessing.

He was older, mid-twenties perhaps. I guessed ex-Army. He was quiet; watchful. He wore cutoff jean shorts frayed just above the knee, lug-soled boots, T-shirts, and a canvas army green jacket. He carried his coffee mug everywhere. His left thumb hooked through the handle and his palm cradled the base. His hair was dark brown, shaggy, and shiny. It fell over his aviator sunglasses and below his ears. He pushed it back behind his right ear before taking a swig from his mug.

————

We'd arrived a week before the camp kids were scheduled to be there in order to get our cabins and the barn ready. My job was to prepare the horse stalls, do general maintenance around the barn, clean tack, and break in the horses as they arrived. The heat and humidity of the Pennsylvania forest made us sweaty and sticky, but the promise of a breeze on damp skin, or the lake water at the end of the day was simple satisfaction. Most of the time I was happily half-covered in a gritty film of musky horse dander and shavings.

I'd taken to wearing a pair of gray running shorts to do the barn work. They were lightweight with built-in panties that I soaked through daily with sweat. Over the course of the summer, they became my favorite shorts. Because of the hard work and all the riding, they'd begun to hang more loosely on my body. I'd begun to like the feel of my hipbones jutting from beneath the cool fabric, and as I walked across the field to the barn in the morning I'd taken to running my hands over my hips and ass. I was beginning to feel contours I liked.

I'd rinse the shorts out in the cabin sink each night, but not before holding them to my face, inhaling my own tangy scent.

Because of the relentless heat, I'd sometimes wear the shorts riding instead of my heavy jeans. I'd squeeze my damp thighs into borrowed suede chaps and zip them down the outside of my legs, tucking the silky ends of the shorts into the suede, which began at my upper thighs. It wasn't a foolproof strategy. In the blazing sun, at a posting trot, the shorts gathered in all my cracks and exposed my bare ass to the hot leather of the saddle. It felt ruinous and delicious all at once.

Sometimes I'd catch Charlie watching from the opposite end of the outdoor ring. He'd lean on the top rail of the fence with his arms crossed and one boot hooked over the bottom rail. On really hot days he wore a red bandana around his forehead, occasionally mopping the sweat from his mustache and beard with the back of his hand.

———

It was a near full moon, and six of us counselors met at the lake to go skinny-dipping. We were already a month into camp, and it was our night off. Mike and Barb, and Belinda and Richie were coupled up by then, which left Charlie and me. I can't remember whose idea the skinny-dipping was, but it seemed like a challenge we were all up for—as if group nakedness was some sort of necessary camp ritual. I was excited and terrified to be naked in front of other people. We stood on the beach in a silhouetted line waiting for the first person to strip and run into the water.

Richie and Belinda shed their clothes quickly and raced ahead splashing and yelling. Someone yelled something about shrinkage. Mike and Barb stripped and followed immediately. I was left standing with Charlie on the beach, fully clothed.

"That a ring on your toe?" he said.

I looked down at my feet, "Yeah, it's been there since high school."

"Won't it come off in the water?"

"Nah."

"Kinky," he said.

I looked at him.

"You going in?" he said.

"Planning on it."

I'd been planning how to gracefully undress with the group so as not to be studied. I both hated and wanted eyes on my body. Now, I felt exposed and singled out. I was fighting an eating disorder, which is to say fighting the myth of having the perfect body, or ever feeling comfortable in the body I had. The binge/purge cycle had intensified freshman year, but I'd begun swimming every day in the natatorium and it was meditative. Water had a way of smoothing everything out and making me feel weightless. At the time, feeling weightless in my body was a goal, but so was the urge to disappear altogether, and I was well on my way. I'd lost nearly thirty pounds.

In what felt like one movement, I pulled my running shorts down, my T-shirt over my head, and unclasped my bra, dropping everything in a heap. I waded into the lake up to my knees and dove in an arc, ass to the moon and the night air. The water felt like silk against my skin. It made my nipples hard. Underwater, I ran my hands over my hips, waist, and erect breasts feeling slim and powerful.

I surfaced, hair plastered to my head, and turned to the beach. "You coming?" I said.

I began swimming to the dock in the middle of the lake, following the others. We formed a dotted line of dark wet heads bobbing in the glimmering water. I heard Charlie wade in, and then a splash. I could sense him following.

The water felt clean and cool against my skin, and I kicked the breaststroke—balls of my feet together, knees out, my body buoyant in the lake water, naked yet hidden. Making it to the dock, I realized Charlie had closed the distance and was right behind me. When I reached up to grab the silver rails of the ladder, his hands fell into place just below mine. I leaned back into his chest and felt an electric jolt of skin-on-skin. His chin grazed my collarbone.

"Help you up?" he said in my ear.

I froze for a second, embarrassed to realize the full view he'd be getting from below. I curved forward and pulled myself up in one motion. I folded myself down near the ladder and stretched out flat on my back, curling my arms behind my head. My heart pounded. My ass and shoulder blades warmed against the dock, my breasts pointed hard at the night sky.

"Nice bush," Richie said.

I tried to punch him but scraped my knuckles on the sandpapery dock.

Charlie pulled himself silently up the ladder. He walked close beside me shaking cold beads of water from his hair. He lay down behind my head where I couldn't see him. I looked up at the moon and crossed my right leg over my left at the ankles. My stomach was flat, and for a moment I admired the indent my hip bones created around the soft flesh of my belly, as if it were a pale lake between low mountains.

———

We talked and laughed, and gossiped about the camp director, whom we agreed probably had a cocaine habit, and about how sad we were for the kids whose parents dropped them there for the entire summer. Someone suggested we lay the backs of our heads on another person's stomach, forming a human chain, so we did. Then someone told a ridiculous joke and our heads bumped up and down from laughter, which caused even more laughter. I don't remember Charlie participating, but I sensed him listening and watching.

In between, I silently marveled at the moon and how it made the lake water roil. I stole glimpses of the others' naked bodies, mostly triangles of dark hair and luminescent breasts, before rolling on my stomach and giving the moon the moon.

———

Back on shore, we toweled off, put our clothes back on, and gathered in the lifeguard shed where they stored the oars, life jackets, buoys, and the thin, fiberglass hulls of sailboats.

Someone had started a fire in an old coffee can with nail holes punched in the side. The shed doors were open; beer cans littered the dirt floor. The others were coupled up with their legs entwined, talking, drinking, and laughing in the flickering light.

I was sitting close to Charlie on the overturned hull of a Minifish. I was in my T-shirt and running shorts, but my bra was still out on the sand. I was shivering, and my hair was wet and beginning to curl.

The other two couples fell to silent kissing. It felt awkward. Charlie leaned closer to me, "Wanna' make out?"

"Mmmmm," I said.

I leaned my right shoulder under his left arm, and settled into his lap facing him. I encircled his waist, sliding my palm up his back under his shirt. "Sorry about my cold hands," I said tracing the jut of each backbone with my fingers and shivering.

Cradling the back of my neck in the crook of his left arm, he pulled me up to meet his mouth. I paused and breathed him in. He kissed me slowly and gently; I tasted the faint trace of a cigarette smoked hours ago. My tongue tracked his mustache where it met the top of his lip.

Our teeth clicked together and I laughed pulling back. "Sorry," I said. I moved deeper into him and his right hand slipped under my shirt and up my ribcage, his thumb tracing the underside of my left breast before he fanned his fingers out, cupping it from the side and swirling his forefinger around my pointed nipple. "You're a handful," he said.

I kissed him deeper and squirmed. Planting my right hand on the sailboat hull for balance, I took my mouth off his and brought my left hand up to his cheek. His still-damp hair was soft, and I lifted my body up to kiss his forehead, working my way slowly down to his eyelids, cheekbones, and chin before burying my face at the indentation at the base of his neck inhaling him. I licked beads of lake water from his hair before searching again for his mouth. His palm was at the small of my back now, pressing me into him. We curled around each other. I'd have kept kissing him like that forever. I felt desirable, lit, devoured.

The shed felt like it was swimming around me. I could hear the whimper and crackle of the tiny can fire, and the others whispering to each other and laughing softly. Here I am, I thought, I'm in my body. I like my body. I like what's being done to my body, and what I'm doing to someone else's body.

Charlie's right hand was now on the soft round of my belly. He moved it slowly down and around toward my ass and down my thigh. He worked his fingers up under my shorts tracing the outline of my hip, mirroring the curve of the panties with his thumb on my goosebumped skin. I couldn't control my wetness. I shuddered and smelled my own embarrassed heat. I let out a nearly inaudible noise, from deep in the back of my throat; the same sound I make now when I hear a delicious poem I want to fuck. He pulled me tighter.

"Let's get outta here," he said.

He stood and extended his hand to help me up. Barefoot and flushed, I tugged my T-shirt down, straightened my shorts, and felt his stare. We went outside to his brown Ford Pinto. I chattered nervously about spending summers tooling around with my friend in her brother's Pinto. "Aren't these the cars with the gas tank that catches fire?" "Do you have any good cassettes?" "What kind of music do you like to listen to?"

When I settled in the front seat, he put the car into gear. "Where do you want to go?" he asked.

"I don't care," I said. "What do you mean?"

"Well, we can't go back to the cabins," he said.

I shrugged.

He looked at me and cocked his head. "Have you ever had sex?" I looked down into my own wet lap.

"God damn, girl" he said. "I'm not going to be your first, but what are you doing kissing someone like that if you had no intentions of following through?"

I looked at his crotch, tented in his jean shorts.

Oh, but I'd had intentions.

I'd spent so much high school time focused on the negatives about my body—hips and thighs that didn't fit traditional Levi's; not having a 24-inch waist like many of my friends; a robust derriere that came between me and wearing Calvin Klein jeans—that I'd never considered I was capable of turning someone on. I didn't realize my body's power back then; or how to use it to give myself pleasure; or that I deserved pleasure; or that deep kissing and heavy petting wasn't an end in itself, but a gateway drug to desire. I was busy punishing myself for existing. I was busy putting food in my mouth out of self-loathing instead of nourishment, and then throwing it up out of shame. I'd wasted many years on the nostalgia that is negative self-talk; on trying to fix my outer self instead of just being myself. I wanted to go back and give my teenaged self a do-over.

Adult me wanted teenaged me to do all the things she didn't have the agency to do back then.

Had I known what I know now, I would have suggested to Charlie that we meet back at the shed after everyone had left. I'd have pushed him down to sit on the overturned Minifish, straddled his hips and leaned his back against the rib of the shed wall. I'd have held his gaze with mine, pulled my T-shirt slowly over my head, leaned back and offered myself up to his hot mouth. He'd hold me behind the shoulder blades and begin kissing me just below my ribs, moving slowly upward. I'd arch my back, put my hands on his knees and let him devour me until we were feverish and breathing hard.

I'd grab a handful of his hair and pull him close. I'd bend forward to meet his mouth, kiss him as if I were surfacing to breathe in the lake, and gently bite his lower lip. I'd curl my fingers into his and place his hands on my body exactly where it felt good. I'd tug his shorts open.

"Please," I'd say, grazing his ear with my lips. "Oh, please."

With my thumb, I'd move aside the panties in my running shorts and slip him inside me, silky and wet. We'd swirl around each other, listening to the lake lap the shore outside. His hands guiding my hips, the water outside reminding us that it always finds its own level.

Babes

Confession

I sit alone at a cocktail party, drinking my gin and tonic and staring into the middle distance. In my peripheral vision, I see Mary Gaitskill break away from a small group and float my way like an apparition. She settles into the chair next to me, which is plush with wing-like arms and red as a power lipstick.

"These remind me of those butterfly chairs from the '60s," I say.

Her limbs are feline, her skin blindingly white. My eyes trace the blue of her carotid that runs like an arterial highway down her neck. It pulses gently below the skin near her clavicle.

The elbow of her right arm rests on her crossed knee, and her left hand moves up to her face, cradling her delicate chin in her palm. I scan her face, so close to mine.

"I want to tell you the story of a doll I had as a child," she says.

This is a commonality between us: dolls. I collect them. Earlier this evening my friends gifted me a Red Riding Hood-like basket with a trio of creepy dolls. The first was a young girl with an alabaster face made of plaster. The second was a baby doll in a red gingham dress. Her eyes blinked as her head rocked back and forth, or they might have if her cloudy left eye wasn't stuck wide open. She had a hole in her mouth where a girl might stick a toy baby bottle. The third had bangs and ponytails made from the kind of white rope you'd use to tie a parcel. Her mouth was painted red and opened in an "O." She reminded me of a Real Doll, the inflatable three-hole masturbatory sex dolls. Her body was soft and stuffed.

Most of my dolls are creepy. Some damaged. Maybe this is the point.

———

I felt like a little girl whose literary godmother had come to sit on the bed. In college, Mary had ensorcelled me with her short story collection *Bad Behavior*. Her novel *Two Girls Fat and Thin* just about saved my early adult life. Now, Mary Gaitskill wanted to tell me a bedtime story. I leaned in and my eyes widened. I'm pretty sure my mouth hung open.

As a young girl, Mary was given a doll named Linda, but she changed its name to Beautiful Sue after she hacked the doll's hair off to the scalp and stripped it naked. She played with the doll for a while, she said, then grew bored and discarded it.

Years later, she found Beautiful Sue while cleaning out her sister's house. Her sister was a hoarder who lived among buried things. Mary unearthed Beautiful Sue and took the doll home with the intent of throwing it away. Instead, she dragged the doll from place to place to place, hiding it in corners, storing it in boxes, or shoving it in the back of a closet. The doll kept materializing. She couldn't seem to bring herself to get rid of it, and yet she wanted to be rid of it. Finally, a friend of Mary's made Beautiful Sue some new clothes, and a

leopard print hat to cover its balding head. Now that she
had proper funeral clothes, the next step was clear: Mary
found a cardboard box, dug a hole in the backyard of a
house she'd rented, and interred Beautiful Sue.

"I feel like she wants me to come back for her," says
Mary. "But I can't be sure I remember exactly where I'd
buried her."

"It's interesting what we bury," I say.

I may or may not have said something about dolls as
fetish objects, and how I use dolls in my visual art to play
with the thorny ways women are objectified, or about the
heartbreak of never being able to escape the clutch of
girlhood. I don't remember the next part of the conversation, frankly. I just remember being lost in the clear
blue of Mary's eyes, and wondering what she was thinking. I don't remember what led her to ask me the next
question.

"What is breaking your heart these days?" Mary asks.
Or maybe it's who?

I want to conjure a good story to deflect the truth sitting fresh on the surface. But the voice in my head says:
"You can't lie to Mary Gaitskill. She'll see right through
your bullshit."

Behind those cat-eye glasses, she even blinks with
agency.

My glasses are cat-eyed too, and suddenly I imagine
we are both felines, growling and rubbing our spines
against different table legs. But more than that, I sense
I am in the Lady Chapel of a medieval church. I light a
candle to the Mary in front of me. My confession spills
out.

"A poet is breaking my heart."

———

246 · MEGAN CULHANE GALBRAITH

I fucked him. I let him fuck me. It was glorious and sad and beautiful, the way he held me. I buried my head in his chest, opened my mouth wide to take him in. I commanded him to bury his cock, his fingers, and his tongue deep inside me, to pull my hair, to bite my lips. I begged him to fuck me deep and hard, and from behind. I invoked God. "Oh my God, yes," I screamed over and over. I purred. I felt powerful, soft, and stuffed. I asked for it. I wanted him to.

He was the second man I'd slept with since ending my marriage of twenty-four years. Our sex was animalistic. We growled and screamed and writhed, licked and nipped, and devoured each other. We spent entire days in bed talking, kissing, reading, and sucking.

"Bite me here," he'd said. "Leave a mark."

One morning, our bodies stacked like spoons, he told me he loved me. I wanted to say it back, but didn't think he meant it the way I needed to hear it. "What does love mean to you?" I asked. His answer was dry as dirt.

I was greedy for him, but he was greedy for all women, so I broke it off. I wasn't interested in being an object, a sex kitten; a toy. I wanted love and long-term. I felt powerful in my need. I left it clean.

Two weeks later, in a pique of exhausted melancholy, I called him for emotional support.

"He told me he tested positive for Herpes," I say. Mary doesn't blink.

———

I want to bury him. I want to inter his smell, his taste, his moans, his love, and my heart, in a box six feet deep in the ground. Who is breaking my heart, indeed?

"I'm awaiting the results of a test I never imagined I'd have to take," I say. "The educator at Planned Parenthood said, 'We don't call if the test is negative.'"

I swear to myself that if this call never comes, I'll never wait for another call from a man.

Mary absorbs my confession like a bruise. "You know," she says, "Your fifties is a great time to be a woman: Fifty is the new thirty."

Then, she leans in further so no one at the party can hear.

"What's the difference between love and herpes?" she asks, her eyes twinkling, their pink lids widening.

"What's the difference?" I ask.

She levels her chin and looks straight into my eyes. Her lips curve into a smile; she shows teeth. I see a hint of fang.

"Herpes lasts forever," she says, throwing her delicate arms above her head like two white flags of surrender.

I wince, but she has a benevolent gleam in her eye. It tells me I have no sin to confess—no bad behavior. I am holy and so is she. I giggle. Her joke feels merciless and merciful for its naked honesty.

I lean forward and we cackle together.

Daddy loved to pose you girls on the red bench he made

Cardioversion

Nancy is carrying *Jane Fonda's Workout* tape under her armpit on our walk through the subdivision from her house to the one she's housesitting. It's 1982. The cover of the VHS shows Jane in leg warmers, gold hoop earrings, and something that looks like a headband around her tiny waist.

———

I don't remember specifically why we are exercising to *Jane Fonda's Workout* in this darkly paneled Connecticut living room, but I'm pretty sure it has to do with getting in shape for boys.

———

Nancy is lithe, blond, and blue-eyed. I am plump, brunette, and blue-eyed. We are not wearing colorful leotards or leg warmers. We are wearing cutoff jean shorts, mismatched sweat socks, and Sheena Easton-style headbands. The point is to get our teenage hearts pumping.

———

If your heart has an irregular (uneven) beat or is beating too fast, cardioversion is a way to restore a regular rhythm. Abnormal heart rhythms are called arrhythmias.

———

My friend texts me to say her husband must go to the hospital for his second cardioversion.

———

Cardioversion is a medical procedure that restores a normal heart rhythm in people with certain types of abnormal heartbeats.

———

I've been talking and texting with my newest lover every day since we met more than a month ago. I've programmed a special ding that makes his texts sound like a dainty bell. It lets me tell them apart from the others.

My heart skips a beat when I hear that pretty sound.

———

Cardioversion is usually performed by sending electric shocks to your heart through electrodes placed on your chest.

———

Nancy has agreed to do *Jane Fonda's Workout* with me because she is one of my best friends. She doesn't need to get thin. Getting thin is my only goal in high school.

Her thighs are lithe, creamy, and smooth. They do not touch. My thighs are also creamy and smooth, but the flesh kisses together at my thighs. In the summer my thighs get sweaty and rub together, which gives me an angry red rash the color of the stripes in Jane's leotard. We called this "chub rub."

Our hearts get pumping fast. I feel as if mine is rubbing against my ribcage.

———

Cardioversion is usually a scheduled procedure that's performed in a hospital. You should be able to go home the same day as your procedure. For most people, cardioversion quickly restores a normal heart rhythm.

———

I get my first period at halftime of a basketball game. Iron-colored blood stains the crotch of my JV cheerleading briefs. The zipper only zipped halfway, so I jerry-rigged the waist of the pleated skirt with a diaper pin. I have a panic attack in the girl's bathroom because I don't know what to do about my period. My friend Wendy hands me a tampon that I don't know how to use.

———

Cardioversion may cause blood clots in your heart to become dislodged, which circulate in the bloodstream and cause life-threatening complications, such as stroke. For some people, cardioversion does not restore a regular heartbeat.

———

The sound I've programmed on my iPhone to make me aware of my calendar appointments sounds similar to the sound I've programmed for texts from my new love interest. I begin to worry that receiving and decoding his passively worded texts has become more a task on my "to do" list. My heart skips and repeats.

———

Cardioversion is usually performed by sending electric shocks to your heart through electrodes placed on your chest.

———

I've been separated from my husband for more than six months now. My heart has begun to regulate itself. Yet it falls into my stomach like a malfunctioning elevator when I see him. I am a hostage to other people's feelings—everyone's emotional support animal. I chart my breath, in and out. I am alive.

———

Cardioversion is performed when your heart is beating ineffectively. It's usually scheduled in advance but is sometimes also done in emergency situations.

———

My paramour and I talk on the phone for hours at a time. We agree we should slow things down. There's infatuation, I say, and there is love. He tells me he loves me, but

I am wary. The agreement is we won't talk or text for a week to give each other space to be whole, to focus on our jobs, our families, and ourselves. "I don't want to be with someone who is not whole," I say. "I don't want someone to put their life aside for me." It was a prescription we'd written for each other. Do NOT call or text for a solid seven days. Within hours he'd texted me "Fuck it. I miss you already." And my heart shocked back into rhythm.

———

Cardioversion is usually used to treat people who have atrial fibrillation or atrial flutter. These conditions occur when the electrical signals that generally make your heart beat at a regular rate don't travel properly through the upper chambers of your heart.

———

In high school, I was always on some diet or another to try to shrink myself into a version of a proper cheer-leader. Once, while babysitting, I discovered a book on the mother's bedside called *Fit for Life*. It advocated fasting for one week, eating only raw fruits and vegetables. I ate only kiwis for seven days, but my heart wasn't into it.

———

Before cardioversion, you may have a procedure called a transesophageal echocardiogram (TEE) to check for blood clots in your heart, which can be dislodged by cardioversion, causing life- threatening complications. You typically can't eat or drink anything for about eight hours before your procedure.

———

It is Day Two of our special diet of not talking or texting and I broke my fast. I requested we be able to send one text and response to each other at bedtime. It took him two and a half hours to respond. "You can text me," he wrote, "but I won't initiate unless I really want to." If I initiated, he said, he might not return my text for a day. "I have renewed energy to see this through," he said.

———

Cardioversion is different from defibrillation, an emergency procedure that's performed when your heart stops or quivers uselessly. Defibrillation delivers more powerful shocks to the heart to correct its rhythm.

———

My friend tells me her husband isn't responding to the cardioversion and they're monitoring him now for a pacemaker.

———

Flat lining is the technical term for when the heart no longer pumps, and a straight line appears on the cardiac machine. The brain can survive for about six minutes after the heart stops.

Daddy loved to pose you girls on the red bench
he made. Courtesy of Michael B. Culhane.

Hold me like a baby

Learning to Mother Myself

I am sitting on the stonewall outside my studio, reading Rebecca Solnit's *The Faraway Nearby*, and thinking about how excited I'd been to get far away from my family. I'd been awarded a month-long writer's residency from The Saltonstall Foundation in Ithaca, New York. It was my first residency, and I had no idea what to expect. What to bring? How to handle the silence? What if I couldn't produce any writing or art?

It never occurred to me that I'd miss my family. I thought I craved solitude, but a month inside my own head was taking its toll. I was awash in self-doubt. I missed my husband, my boys, and my stepdaughter. I missed the dogs that I'd cursed daily for their endless silent pleading, "Let me in, let me out, let me in, let me out." I didn't know how to be still with myself because it seemed there was so little stillness at home.

I looked up from the book and noticed a delicate snakeskin pinned beneath dead daylily leaves in the dirt to my left. The snakeskin was preserved in its entirety, from head to tail, not a rip or a tear. Its mouth was open as if it was mid-strike, and I could see the dark jeweled ovals where the snake's eyes had been. It was nearly two feet

258 · MEGAN CULHANE GALBRAITH

long, a garter snake most likely, and the perfect embodiment of the reptile itself rendered like a tissue-thin sepia-toned X-ray.

The sight of it gave me pause. Here I was jumping out of my skin, trying to shed a skin, or get comfortable with the skin I was in. Back home I was a mother, wife, and daughter. I was struggling to leave those identities behind. Perhaps I was struggling to find myself again and begin anew.

I tried not to tear the snakeskin as I pried it out from under the desiccated leaves.

Touching it excited and terrified me. Why? As a child, I'd loved to play outside. In fact, one of my fond memories was of capturing a garter snake and allowing it to slither through my fingers and across the palms of my hands. I must have been five or six years old at the time. I'd had no qualms about picking that snake up. I was a curious child, without fear or pretense. What power I'd had back then. The snake was terrified of me.

Now, age and time have reversed our roles. I wasn't frightened of the snake, but by the husk the snake left behind. Where had my curious child-self gone? Where was my sense of wonder and discovery? I'd hoped to use this time to get out into nature, to avail myself of long walks in the woods, explore the area gorges again, and take long hot baths.

Instead, I felt pinned down like that snake's former skin, terrified of being outside, of Lyme disease, the Zika virus, or getting lost in the woods unable to find my way back.

I'd worked in Ithaca almost three decades ago. Cornell was my first real job after graduating from Penn State, and I'd gone on to careers in Troy, New York. Why had it taken me three times as long as Odysseus to return?

I could hear the siren song of my children, who were home plundering my refrigerator for food. I was being tested to sit with my own grief and shame. I'd been given the gift of food, friendship, a bed, quiet time, and space to write. I sensed this snakeskin was an omen, but to what? Had the twenty years I'd spent nurturing my family denatured the childish curiosity out of me? Could I learn to be a good mother to my child self?

———

There'd been an extended drought in Ithaca. The roaring waterfalls and gorges that are its natural gems had been reduced to trickles. The mayor had announced a drought emergency. We were in strict conservation mode, and so was I, it seemed.

As a child, I remember that garter snake leaving an intense musk all over my hands. It stunk like a mixture of stale urine and fresh feces. I'd dropped the snake and cupped my hands to my face inhaling deeply and recoiling. I did this multiple times trying to identify the scent mixture. Then, I ran inside to my mother and raised my hands to her face. She flinched and told me the smell was the snake's defense mechanism.

I forced myself to pry this snakeskin up and out of the dirt. I wanted to reconnect with the curious child I'd been, and to allay my adult fears that I'd passed along to my children. How could I have let myself become so fearful?

———

As I sat writing, I realized it was August 5, my mother's birthday. She would have been seventy-six, had she not died nearly twenty years ago. I couldn't run to her any-more to help me identify odd stinks, or to ask her questions about the kids, or for comfort.

You'd think my grief would have subsided by now, but it hadn't. Rather, it had accumulated over the years and settled into parts of my body wearing me like a second skin. Grief pins you down.

———

The days are long and hot here. I feel slightly reptilian sitting in my air-conditioned studio, and guilty for looking out my window over the field to the view of the mountains and the horizon. I should be out there playing, running barefoot, picking up snakes, and throwing rocks into the pond, like I did when I was a child.

Within the first week, the rains came in torrents that greened the grass and refilled the aquifers. I took the long, hot bath I'd been craving. I filled the tub with water as hot as I could stand, and added bubbles infused with Argan oil, which moisturizes and nourishes the skin. I eased myself down and sat there while my skin turned bright red from the intense heat. Sweat poured down my face and steamed my reading glasses. I suppose soaking in that tub, sweating the dirt out of my pores, was a way of shedding my skin. Baths are enjoyable until you realize you're sitting in a hot steamy swirl of your own dead skin cells. I was basically stewing in my own juices.

When I stood up, I imagined that the surface tension of the water was drawing up the dead cells and cementing them on to my clean self. Reverse metamorphosis, the opposite of growth.

———

Snakes shed their skin to accommodate growth; humans don't shed our skin, we grow into it.

I longed for the out-of-body experience I imagined that snake must have felt after sloughing off the husk of its former self. I wanted to glide away to a quiet, cool place where I waited out the heat of the day and emerged replenished and ready.

Mom. Courtesy of Michael B. Culhane.

Birth Mother/Daughter reunion,
Fitzpatrick Manhattan Hotel, 1996

Timepiece

My caseworker, Jackie, at Catholic Charities told me it had taken only one phone call to find Ursula, whose last employer had been at an arts council in Toronto.

"I remember her talking about a daughter she had out there somewhere," said the man who had answered the phone there before offering up Ursula's phone number in Scotland.

"That was one of the easiest searches I've ever done," Jackie said.

Ursula and I wrote letters to each other and sent them via airmail. We talked on the telephone. It was the '90s, and the Internet and email were both in their infancy. She was an administrator for an arts council in Scotland at the time, and she was open to being "found," said Jackie, who'd carefully brokered the introduction.

I'd come to find out that I wasn't a secret in her life, but rather that I'd been quite the cocktail party story.

Urusla arranged for us to meet in New York City at The Fitzpatrick Manhattan hotel in midtown because she'd wanted us to be close to The Guild of the Infant Saviour, which had operated at 225 East 52nd Street until 1976.

We spent a long fall weekend in New York. We walked the city streets. We talked. We smoked, and drank red wine. I pumped breast milk for my son and stored it in the tiny hotel room refrigerator. We ate room-service hamburgers that first night, and she'd brought a bottle of champagne, which chilled on its side in the fridge next to my breast milk. The neighborhood had changed so much, Ursula said.

We walked down the street where she'd remembered The Guild had been located. We stood on the sidewalk looking up. The original row of Italianate brownstones had been razed and the Hungarian Consulate built in its place. Standing there on the pavement she told me we were Hungarian. She pointed to a corner where she and "the girls" used to buy their cigarettes at a long-since-gone bodega.

"We had to walk out in pairs," she said. "The women who ran the home kept a basket of cheap rings by the door. They told us to take one and wear it on our left hand when we went outside so that it would look like we were married."

One night during our visit, Ursula took me to a Chinese food restaurant—a modest little place on the Lower East Side with Formica tables, the ubiquitous waving Lucky Cat, and bright red curtains. It was near one of the first apartments she'd had in the city, she said. She'd lived there with a bunch of single girls after I'd been born. She said she'd felt free and alive.

"I remember all of us rushing back to the apartment on Thursday nights to watch *The Waltons*," she said. "We'd order pizza, watch TV, and cry. I always thought I'd like to have a family like that."

Over hot green tea, dumplings, and moo-shu pork she asked, "Do you like silver or gold?" and then worked her hand deep into her bag and produced a piece of jewelry—a gold locket suspended on a watch fob. "I saved this for you in case we ever met," she said.

She began to tell me the story of Junior, of paperboard boxes, and of a gilded moment in time to which we each seemed to have a tenuous claim. I listened closely. It felt like she was telling me my first bedtime story.

————

Robert Gair's watch fob is made of a mix of rose and 24-carat gold. Pocket chains of this sort are typically attached to a timepiece like a pocket watch, but this one holds only a hinged locket. On one side of the locket is an onyx intaglio of Ares, the Greek God of war and masculinity; on the other side are the initials "R" and "G" in ornate Victorian typeface. It is a piece of mourning jewelry I wear now as a necklace—an heirloom of my reclaimed past.

Inside the locket was a hank of Junior's blond hair, curled twice around itself under a piece of delicate glass. The story goes that Junior was the first-born illegitimate son of Ursula's grandmother, Vera Fitzmaurice Weed, who had been sixteen years old.

Vera's older cousin Helen (Fitzmaurice) married Robert Gair, and they adopted Junior "into the family," which was common in the mid-1900s as a way to conceal illegitimacy and deal with the shame associated with a bastard child. While this type of adoption kept things in the family, I wondered how many other family secrets had been kept. As an adoptee I disdain secrets.

Junior had been in his early twenties and a pilot-in-training in the Army Air Force when his B-17 Bomber exploded in mid-air over Texarkana.

As we got to know each other, I peppered Ursula with questions. These were some of my favorite times: us sitting together on her screened-in porch in Florida, drinking cocktails and me listening to her stories.

"Your great-grandmother Vera made a deathbed confession to my Uncle Dickie Weed that Junior was the illegitimate son she gave up for adoption," Ursula said. "Can you believe I had an uncle named Dick Weed?"

———

Helen (Fitzmaurice) married into the Gair fortune and a wholly different life from her cousin Vera. In Ursula's words, "They were rich, and we were poor." It was rumored that Vera had had three other out-of-wedlock births before marrying my great-grandfather, Howard Dewey Weed, whom I was told was also a foundling, abandoned at the Chicago World's Fair. I researched this, and out of 10,000 children reported lost or abandoned in Chicago during the fair in 1893, there was one boy whose parents never came back for him. Could he have been my biological great-grandfather?

I began researching Ursula's story in great gulps; unwinding it in the same way I'd wanted to unravel the strands of Junior's hair. Now that I'd found her, I wanted her story to be my story too. I'd find a truth covered in glass and concealed within a fog of memory.

Over the course of many years, I pressed Ursula with questions and asked for further clarification. Uncle Dick was still alive. Could she ask him about the deathbed confession? She did.

Later still, she reversed course. The deathbed confession had been wrong, she said, Vera hadn't had *any* illegitimate children but rather, likely, several self-administered abortions. My great-grandfather hadn't been found at *the* Chicago World's Fair, she said, but had rather "worked at *a* World's Fair." Her blunt tone made me feel as if she was blaming me for believing the story she'd told me in the first place.

I'm fascinated by the scrim of memory; how and why we remember what we do in the way we do. Memory can be a lacey veil, a different lens through which to see a past, and a coping mechanism for trauma. Family folklore recounts events as a way of passing down a common family identity and as a creative expression of a collective past. It is raw experience distilled and transformed into bedtime stories, photo albums, family heirlooms, heirlooms, recipes, and traditions. Over time our stories become polished, embellished, and reshaped according to various fears, needs, and desires. None of this is wrong or untrue. None of this is bad. As families reshape themselves through birth, adoption, marriage, divorce, tragedy, triumph and death, our oral histories change as well. The same story can be told and retold by a different family member in myriad ways. Facts and stories that do not enhance the image of the family, for example, often go unsaved and untold. The painful ones may be edited or removed entirely from the fragile strands of the family narrative, and those who choose to speak of the pain often become estranged.

Aren't we all unreliable narrators?

As an adoptee, I wanted to track down every last detail I could find of Ursula's stories, not to simply verify the parts of my narrative that may have been lost to time, but to understand where I fit within a past I hoped to reclaim. There were more indications of truth in her original memories than there were of falsehoods.

———

I came across Gair Building No. 7, now called The Clock Tower Building, in DUMBO Brooklyn, while researching my newfound genealogy and Junior's.

Robert Gair was described by his biographer H. Allen Smith as "a grizzled giant of a man, as handsome as a portrait and as stubborn in his convictions as Toscanini." Gair had been a Union Army commander with the Seventy-Ninth Highlanders of the Ninth Corps of the Army of the Potomac in the Civil War. He commanded the regiment at the siege of Knoxville and Spottsylvania. Of his regiment, only 200 of the original 1,087 survived the war.

Sixty days after he'd mustered out of the Army, Gair founded the paper company that made him his fortune. His son George inherited the business and passed it on to his wife Helen, who passed it to Vera's daughter, my grandmother Helen.

In 1879 Gair stumbled upon a way to score and fold paper into boxes. One of his machines malfunctioned, and instead of cutting the ream, as was intended, it creased the paper. That accident transformed an industry. Gair realized he could use his machines to score paper, which meant it could be folded into three dimensions, efficiently making paper cartons and containers. He retooled his machines, filed a patent, and birthed the commercial packaging industry in America.

"Gair's box, a cheap, light alternative to wood, became the swaddling clothes of our metropolitan civilization," wrote Lewis Mumford in his introduction to "Robert Gair: A Study."

Crackers that had previously grown stale and soggy in their unsanitary cracker barrels could now be sold fresh, crispy, and sealed in paperboard boxes made by Gair. The National Biscuit Company was one of his first clients, and

Gair even had a hand in the branding of Uneeda Biscuits. Other companies that produced everything from Brillo pads to coffee to soap began to flock to him to package their products.

"More than any other personality, except that of Roebling, the creator of the Brooklyn Bridge, Robert Gair symbolically dominates the Brooklyn waterfront,'" wrote Mumford.

Gair's paper plant comprised six blocks on the Brooklyn waterfront—a total of seven huge buildings—and the area was named "Gairville." In 1914, Gair built The Clock Tower at 1 Main Street between Water and Plymouth Streets in Brooklyn. He built ten structures there— a small city—including a stable for horses, a powerhouse (which houses the bookstore The Powerhouse Arena), and a pier where ships could dock. The vestiges of the old railway lines he laid are embedded in the cobblestone streets today—I walk them like a balance beam when I visit. Gair seemed to have thought of everything in his self-sufficient, self-contained industrial city. He built tunnels under the streets between his buildings, and aerial bridges so his employees could do their jobs efficiently.

Gairville remained a waterfront industrial area for nearly a century until the 1970s when it was renamed DUMBO—an acronym for Down Under the Manhattan Bridge Overpass. The clock and its four-story, four-sided faces still overlook New York Harbor, and both the Brooklyn and Manhattan Bridges. Gair's name is chiseled over the side entrance of the Clock Tower Building, among others.

In its time—The Clock Tower was the tallest building in the world to be constructed of reinforced concrete. It is now the centerpiece of the most expensive neighborhood in Brooklyn.

As manufacturing increased, so did the workforce in Brooklyn. Spurred by jobs that Gair's business provided (nearly 3,000 in its heyday), an influx of workers began settling in and around the Brooklyn waterfront.

The Clock Tower and the other Gair buildings are protected now by listings on the National Historic Register. The Clock Tower no longer serves as a paper manufacturing plant. It is now one of the most expensive residences in DUMBO and home to Etsy, Inc. The guts of the original 14-foot clocks are gone; the clocks were replaced with different mechanisms and still keep time. The Clock Tower's four incandescent faces are now windows to an $18 million penthouse that was once named *Esquire's* Ultimate Bachelor Pad before it was purchased by the actress Anne Hathaway.

Looking back, it's apparent that the Clock Tower is a larger version of the watch-fob Ursula gave me. Both represent time gone by, and complication, and missing pieces, and something lost and found.

I wanted to travel back in time to meet Junior and the Gairs. Instead, I stitched together a family story to figure out where it intersects with mine. As you can imagine, there are a lot of moving parts.

———

I was struggling with the genealogical facts of Ursula's story, so I began poking into my biological lineage at the New York Public Library. There, in the thousands of hardbound birth records, I located a birth listing for a "Male—Fitzmaurice" to a Vera Fitzmaurice in 1917, which was likely Junior's birth year. I could not find subsequent census listings for a son who had lived with Vera or her family. There is no trace of him, and it seems he never lived with her again, which leads me to believe

Ursula's initial story is accurate; that Vera surrendered her first-born son.

I can't find Junior's original birth certificate, and I don't have access yet to my own either. This is where information dead-ends for adoptees. We operate on shreds of stories and slivers of fact. We are denied information that natural born children have access to. We collide with the paradox of having to prove our identity without having any proof of our identity. We are two people in one body.

———

Helen Fitzmaurice Gair married into a wholly different life from Vera's—a life of privilege, wealth, and (in the end) tragedy. Ursula described her family—our family—as "blue-collar working poor." Her father was a factory worker, and the family lived with Ursula's paternal grandparents in what she called the "crazy Hungarian boarding house," which her grandparents ran in South Norwalk, Connecticut. They lived there for years, she said, until her sister was born and her parents had saved enough money to get a GI mortgage, which allowed them to buy the small Cape Cod house in the Strawberry Hill section of Norwalk, that happened to be less than two miles from the home on Muffin Lane into which I was adopted years later.

Vera named her daughter (my grandmother) Helen (Gair) Weed, after the woman who'd adopted her bastard boy, Helen (Fitzmaurice) Gair. Ursula told me it was homage to Helen raising Vera's son. Would Vera have named her first-born after Helen, otherwise? Why else would Helen have left her entire estate to Ursula's mother?

Ursula said she'd saved Gair's watch fob and locket because it bound Junior and me, two adoptees, together across time. For me it was an object with umbilical pull, with a deep resonance to a specific time in history; a talisman that reminded me I was not the only illegitimate child in the family.

How could I feel so nostalgic about an object? Ursula had wanted me to have the watch fob, but more importantly the story that went with it. Yet, here she was contradicting that story. I felt confused and tender. I began to feel as if my own past was gaslighting me.

———

As I tried to move deeper into my history, the story of the clock tower and the watch fob kept time right along with me, pulling me forward minute by minute.

———

The central figures in my narrative are all fallen women: Women who had illegitimate children, who were "trouble," and who were sent away to Convent School and unwed mother's homes. They were mothers who couldn't mother their own children, or wouldn't, or who were shamed because of the shame they brought to the family.

Society has many different names for such women— hussy, slut, whore, barren, loose, frigid, useless—and names for the children they bore—illegitimate, foundling, orphan, waif, indigent, friendless, and adopted.

———

George and Helen Gair were Society Blue Bloods. They were listed on the Social Register, had residences at 375 Park Avenue (now the site of the Seagram Building), and a summer estate called "Gairellen" on Shippan Point in Greens Farms, Connecticut, an exclusive beach-front community that juts like a forceful chin into Long Island Sound. They hosted royalty, diplomats, and theater stars at Gairellen or on their yacht, *Gairlee*. Junior, the tow-headed boy born to my unwed great-grandmother seemed to complete the family picture.

Ursula made what she called a "Family Album," which included photos of her as a baby in diapers and at many stages of her life before she gave birth to me, and afterward. The Family Album also included photos of my biological family, and a photo of our reunion in New York, which she did not grant me permission to use here.

She also gave me scrapbooks that had belonged to Helen. From the photos, it seemed Junior had the best of everything: private school at Perkiomen Prep, yachting lessons, hunt club, a standard poodle, and lavish birthday parties with society's upper crust. But those scrapbooks also included poems and stories Junior had written in tender handwriting that seemed filled with loneliness. One, titled "White Sails," describes a sea cottage, waves lapping, and a solitary little boy playing in the sand before going off to sleep in a small white bed.

Junior was fifteen years old at the time he wrote that poem and was away at boarding school. Photos Ursula gave me from that time show his parents were on lavish steamer trips to Cairo, Egypt, and Venice, Italy, among other places.

Intra-family adoptions were not uncommon in the 1920s, and I found myself researching my newfound lineage in great gulps; claiming relatives I never knew I had, seeing my image manifested in their zaftig Hungarian bodies, and figuring out where I fit within a high society history that seemed as elusive to me as it was for Ursula.

When she told me her stories, Ursula was careful to stress that Helen "married into the Gair family" and that "you are related to them by marriage": as if we were not part of that family at all, but neighbors who lived on the wrong side of the tracks.

Junior died when he was twenty-three years old. His death came just three years after his father, George, died at Gairellen. I don't have a photo of him at that age—but I do have a photo of the wreckage of his plane—so I imagine him instead: blond hair, close-cropped in a 2nd lieutenant haircut, tall and broad with shoulders that taper to a sculpted waist and the shiny brass of his Army-issued belt buckle. Maybe he had an aquiline nose that pitched slightly to the left like I am told my great-grandfather's did: like mine does, and my son Sam's.

———

I wear the locket on special occasions. When I do it takes on the warmth of my body as it hangs in the divot of my throat: the suprasternal notch. The gold radiates warmth on my skin. I imagine Junior close to my heart as my secret cousin, many times removed. Every now and then I wonder what stories we'd have told each other if I were able to travel back in time.

———

In addition to inheriting the Shippan Point estate, Ursula's mother inherited Helen Gair's jewelry—platinum tiaras, diamond brooches, heavy gold bracelets—and handfuls of Continental Can stock (Gair Paper merged with Continental Can in 1956). Ursula told me she remembered her mother readying Gairellen to sell after

Helen's death in the 1950s. They couldn't afford to even heat the place, she said, and not knowing the value of the objects in the estate, her mother had rolled up expensive Persian rugs and other items and sent them off to the Goodwill. I gasped.

"Well, what did she know?" Ursula said. "I remember her saying they were ratty and old."

To pay bills, Ursula told me her mother sold off the rest of the estate. The jewelry was kept under lock and key and sold piecemeal over many years.

"I remember Mom going to the safe deposit box every now and then for another piece of jewelry, a tiara or something, when a big bill was due," Ursula said. "She'd take the train into New York and sell the stuff at Van Cleef & Arpels, or someplace, just to keep us in groceries."

I called Van Cleef & Arpels. They keep impeccable records, but they had no record of any purchase of Helen Gair's jewelry. Possibly, my grandmother pawned some of the jewels and used the proceeds to send teenaged Ursula to convent school.

When Ursula described her time in that convent school, she softened her memories.

"It wasn't as bad as it was in the movie *The Magdalene Sisters*," she said, "but it was pretty bad."

———

In 1989, after Ursula's mother died, Helen's remaining jewelry was divided between her and her sisters. Ursula called it "The Big Grab." The previously vast collection of jewelry had been winnowed down to eight items: a 23-carat blue star sapphire ring; a 10-mm pearl and 1-carat diamond ring; diamond rings weighing 11 carats and

4 carats apiece; a 2-carat diamond brooch; a "Roaring '20s" 2.5-carat ladies diamond watch; a heavy 24-carat gold link bracelet; and Gair's watch fob and locket.

Her older sister had argued that the jewelry should go to the grandchildren—hers. But Ursula countered that she too had a daughter, although she couldn't have been sure we ever would meet. She'd wanted the locket, she told me, precisely because of the adoption story that accompanied it.

———

Great works of literature, including fables and folktales, are constructed with orphaned or abandoned narrators: think Jane Eyre, Pip, Rapunzel, Frodo Baggins, Oliver Twist, and Cinderella. In these Bildungsroman, the waifs escape abuse, inherit unknown fortune, free themselves from imprisonment, destroy a ring, and find their authentic selves (and sometimes a prince). The narrators ask for more, overcome poverty, save the Shire, and uncover secrets on a self-directed journey that leads them to their true heritage and happiness.

In reconstructing a family history for myself, I am fascinated by how strong an effect objects have on me. Maybe this explains my undying love of thrift and antique stores where I can paw through and marvel at other people's nostalgia. Touching things others have held makes me feel connected across time. I view artifacts, particularly family heirlooms, as imbued with protective qualities. The fact that Ursula had saved this watch fob and locket was meaningful because it was against her grain to save things. I'd come to learn from her that her habit as an adult was to jettison books, clothing, objects, and other personal effects in her many adult moves: New

York to Florida, to Toronto, to Scotland, to Texas, then back to Florida to name a few.

Her mother turned family heirlooms into cash perhaps as a way of outrunning poverty. She seemed to have passed that unsympathetic view on to Ursula who'd also pawned, sold, or bartered anything just to get by. Once, she told me she'd had gold fillings in her teeth removed so she could sell the gold so she and her then-husband could eat while they were living in tents on an artist's commune in Canada.

Every heirloom Ursula has given me has also come with the caveat: "If you ever get desperate, you can always sell it."

Yet she kept this watch fob. She'd kept it for me.

She said she has one more item saved for me—the pearl and diamond ring—but she's keeping it, she said, as a hedge against an uncertain future.

———

I imagine George and Helen Gair must have been infertile. Helen was said to have been a Ziegfeld Girl, although I can find no evidence of this. Thanks to her stage career, Ursula said, Helen had access to a pregnancy cage—a simulated belly used in theater productions. Because George had inherited the Gair Paper Company from his father, he made frequent and lengthy business trips to Europe.

Helen's scrapbook shows evidence of many steamer trips. In one of the photos, the couple is smiling on the deck of the SS *Conte Biancamano*. Helen is pictured in a tailored wool coat with fur at the collar and sensible heels. George is in a top hat with a cane. I imagine her sporting a fake belly, waving to her society friends from the upper deck. I imagine Vera below in steerage, with her barely showing baby bump. After a stay in Europe, George and Helen returned with George West Gair Jr., the apple of their eye. Vera may have returned home with a flat belly, and her reputation intact.

In one of the Family Album photographs, George sits on an iron patio chair next to an elaborately landscaped in-ground pool on Shippan Point. He wears a swimsuit, the paunch of his stomach straining a wide-striped tank top. He is barefoot, and his long, white legs are tucked under the chair. A severe middle part cuts through his salt and pepper hair, which is slicked back behind Dumbo-sized ears. His arms are so long that his elbows seem to touch the top of his thighs, and his thin lips curl into a wry smile.

His wife Helen stands behind him, and next to her is my grandmother, her namesake, Helen (Gair) Weed. Both Helens are posing in bathing suits leaning over George's chair. Everyone is smiling like one big happy family. My grandmother's hair is dyed platinum blond. It is bobbed and combed into a side wave that shines in the sun. She could be Ursula's twin. The date, 1935, is written in loopy cursive under the picture. She and George would have been married for nearly twenty-five years. Junior is not in the picture, nor is he in any of the photographs. He was seventeen by then and likely still attending boarding school.

I can see the family resemblance between the Helens, Ursula, and me. I think I see familiar traces of my boys in George's face too: his height, stance, and broad shoulders. He was related by marriage, so this is me willfully projecting these traits because I can. This is what adoptees do, it seems. We try to see ourselves in the faces of others.

—————

I'd never thought to question why it took nearly six months to adopt me, or why my birth certificate had been dated two years after my birth date. It was only when I methodically plotted my first year on a paper calendar—birthday, adoption month, and birth certificate date of issue—that I realized the many months that were unaccounted for. Where had I gone?

Dad had romantic ideas, "You were with the nuns." Mom's early statement to teenage me seemed prophetic, "I don't think you were picked up much," she'd said. "I think they left you lying there in your crib." Ursula was revisionist. "I signed you out of the home on weekends to make a go of it. I would bring you back to my apartment in New York City and try to take care of you."

These stories, it turns out, were versions of a truth. Mom's was perhaps the closest to reality; I likely hadn't been picked up much in that foster home. Ursula's story was probably a fabrication, although birth mothers had up to six months to decide whether they wanted to keep the baby or not. My foster home, I'd learned, was in New Fairfield, Connecticut, nearly a two-hour trip by train and bus from New York City by today's standards. I question that she'd have been able to travel that distance to bring me back to her apartment. Instead, she'd likely invented a memory that consoled her and implied that I wasn't unloved or unwanted.

It took time for me to figure out the right questions to ask, and of whom. Only when I began inquiring at Catholic Charities, the agency that facilitated my adoption, did the story of my early life begin to fall into place.

I'd talked to a different caseworker at Catholic Charities just as she was going on maternity leave. Maybe she empathized with me because she was expecting her own baby at the time, but she agreed to send me items and information from my records despite the fact that adoptee's files are legally sealed and the information is confidential.

"I'm not supposed to send this stuff to you so if anyone asks, you didn't get it from me," she'd said.

A week or so later I received an envelope from Catholic Charities with a photo and handwritten notes on yellow-lined paper. The caseworker wrote that I had been in a foster home during those unaccounted-for months. John and Gertrude Schimansky lived in New Fairfield, Connecticut, and "opened their home to children from 1959–77," she wrote. "During that time period, they cared for approximately seventy-five children. I believe there were two other children in the home during your stay there, along with their own children."

I slipped a 3x5 photo out of the envelope and held it in my hands. It was the earliest picture I had of myself. I figured I must have been about four months old. That period in my life is lost time. Holding that faded Polaroid was like uncovering a piece of buried treasure. I turned it over, and "Gabriella" was written in the top left corner in careful blue penmanship. I broke into tears.

In the photo, I am atop a dining room table in a wire bouncy seat looking directly at the camera. My eyes have a searching look—half blank, half hopeful. The table is covered with a floral tablecloth in Harvest Autumn Gold, a mustardy color popular in the '60s. There is a pack of cigarettes, a clear glass ashtray, and that morning's paper. I am dressed in a white terry cloth sleeper. The snaps are straining around my stomach, and I am clasping my fingers across my chest. It looks as though I am wringing my hands.

In photos I have of me with my adoptive parents, my mom, Roberta, is holding me in the crook of her arm, or helping me stand on toddler's legs, or balancing me on her knee wearing her Gamma Sigma Sigma sweatshirt. Or else she is pushing me on the swing in the backyard: the one that looked like a wooden milk crate suspended from a galvanized chain. My dad is usually behind the camera, snapping pictures and posing us. Mom is smiling her lipsticked smile, bent over at her delicate waist so her shoulders are next to mine. Her arms seem to always be outstretched. Her face is finely boned, and she looks like Audrey Hepburn. I am chubby with a crooked mouth. I look nonplussed.

Mom and I looked nothing alike. Yet there she was, reminding me of who was really holding me up.

If you lay photos of Ursula and me side-by-side at the same young age you can't tell one of us from the other. This is a phenomenon I don't take for granted as an adoptee. I now see myself in the faces of my boys, and in my grandsons. They are my progeny and my heritage all at once. Among the photos in "Our Family Album" was a black and white image of Ursula in a bathing suit on the beach in Wellfleet, Maine. She is holding an inner tube and standing in front of a white clapboard house on a dune.

"That is not our beach house," she said. "We were poor. We could never have afforded a house like that."

I dig up a photo of myself that I know by heart. In the picture, I too am standing on the beach at my grandparents' house, but on Bell Island in Rowayton, Connecticut. My cousins and I spent every summer weekend at that house. We dug for clams with Grampy and his cigar-chomping friend Nick Bredice, watered the island plants with Grammy, and hung the American flag on the pole across from their house without letting it touch the ground. We rowed the dinghy out to the pimple of land in the swamp out back that Grampy called Treasure Island to search for pirate treasure. We shoved fiddler crabs down each other's bathing suits.

In comparing the two photographs, I nearly fell off my chair the similarities were so striking. Ursula and I could have been twins had we not been separated by nineteen years. We had the same boyish haircut as if our mothers had put a mixing bowl on our heads and trimmed around it; the same physical frame (slight scoliosis, rounded belly, fleshy upper arms, thighs that rubbed together); the same sun-squinty expression, and nearly identical bathing suits. Looking at that photo, I felt transported back in time.

Aside from my boys, it was the first time I recognized myself in someone else. It was comforting and eerie, like seeing a friendly ghost.

———

My parents did not keep my adoption a secret. I was their first child. My arrival was celebrated and documented in a pink, padded book embossed with the words "An Adopted Child's Memory Book." I had a spaniel named Mignon, a Shetland pony named Dashaway, an heirloom white christening gown, and photos documenting my every move from my "flower sniffing expression" to Dad posing me like a doll in every conceivable way. Mom had

Scotch-taped a lock of hair from my first haircut, and included a tidy, handwritten list of the gifts I had received and who brought them.

Early Callers and Gifts to Welcome YOU to OUR House:

> Susan Devine with a sterling fork + spoon set
> Anne Devine + family with a baby gold bracelet
> Uncle Joey with a pink corduroy set and a musical turtle
> Grandma + Grandpa Rysz with this book
> Grandma and Grandpa Culhane with money for your bank and to buy you a crib and some clothes
> The English Dept. at Rippowam sent you an infant seat, and the Social Committee sent you a cute pink-and-white checked sunsuit.
> "Peckie" gave you your first silver spoon and a training cup.
> Aunt Ellie and Uncle Teke sent an oval sterling silver frame.

I received two sterling spoons, which prompted my husband at the time to tease that I was born with two silver spoons in my mouth.

Through adult eyes, this list of objects brought to me by my new family highlights how far I'd come economically. I'd been born in a charity hospital in Hell's Kitchen to an unwed mother and adopted into an upper-middle-class family. These are the upwardly mobile economics of adoption; babies are adopted into families with means as measured by (in my case) Catholic Charities. I tried but couldn't obtain the paperwork from my adoption file that contained the questions my parents had to answer during their "adoption home study." A caseworker explained to me that they centered on finances, economic means of raising the baby, questions of religion and education, and motivation to adopt.

I did watch a 1960s documentary called *The Chosen Child,* narrated by John Chancellor of *NBC News* to better get a sense of what my parents went through. It follows couples—all white, all heterosexual—through their home study and selection to become adoptive parents.

"From a very large group of applications 'near perfect' parents can be found," Chancellor narrates. "And 'near perfection' is what these [caseworkers] demand in their job of protecting and providing for their wards, the children. These kind ladies are tough reckoners."

———

When we first met in New York City, I brought my Adopted Child's Memory Book to show Ursula who marveled at the list of gifts and remarked on the social class of my parents who seemed to her to have means and connections. Adoption is now, and always has been, an issue of money. Adoptable children are never adopted into families without the "proper resources." The socioeconomics favor upper-middle-class and wealthy adoptive parents.

My birth mother and her family had neither connections nor money. My adoptive parents had both. Pop Pop was a well-known banker and lawyer in Norwalk, Connecticut, and Momops was a registered nurse. They had a powerful ally in Walter W. Curtis, head of the Roman

Catholic Diocese of Bridgeport, which was the town in which the adoption agency was located.

———

Growing up, I never thought to question my adoptive parents as to why there weren't any newborn pictures of me. It was as if, photographically, I had sprung up a fully formed toddler able to balance on my mother's knee. Oh, I was adorable, my parents told me. Among other things, I had my own swing suspended from a beam in the living room where, Mom said, I pumped away happily singing "Georgy Girl" by The Seekers.

> *Hey there, Georgy girl*
> *Swinging down the street so fancy-free*
> *Nobody you meet could ever see the loneliness there*
>   *inside of you*

Mom always told me I could keep myself busy for hours in my playpen making necklaces and bracelets by connecting and disconnecting Fisher-Price Snap Beads. I realize now that I must have been used to entertaining myself because of the time I'd likely spent alone in the foster home. Out of necessity and survival, I had learned to be self-contained at an early age. I am unsure what to do with these numb feelings, or the sadness that accompanies them.

The act of photographing is about being looked at, not seen. A photograph is a medium that processes someone else's memory of the object being photographed. It is someone else's lens and therefore creates a form of distancing that seems at once both intimate and detached. It's a form of nostalgia that begs the question of the picture taker as much as the person who is being photographed. Photographs are a way of stopping time.

Like many adoptees, I have a lively and imaginative internal life—one that I don't share with many people. I'd always wanted my photographic image to align with the one I have of my inner self, but the two never seemed to square. It was as if I was *beside* myself, not *in* myself, and I could never seem to wrest the two separate ideals of "me" into a corporeal whole. When I saw that first photograph myself, nearly thirty years after it had been taken, it made me feel real.

Hey there, Georgy Girl
There's another Georgy deep inside
Bring out all the love you hide and, oh, what a
*   change there'd be*
The world would see a new Georgy Girl
Wake up, Georgy Girl

———

Time is a paradox that can alter a story depending on how a person chooses to tell it. Time and trauma affect a person's ability to recall details, or to alter them into a palatable story that—like scar tissue—heals over a wound.

I wish I could jump back and forth in time: pausing, rewinding, and fast forwarding through parts of my life: both for the obvious Butterfly Effect and the certainty that comes with such naked omniscience. I want to be able to hover over myself as actor *and* observer, character *and* narrator, situation *and* story.

To experience the world nineteen years apart and under different circumstances from my birth mother is the reason I have so many questions for her. How do

I make peace with seeing my reflection in her? Is she mirror or lens? After all this time, what if I dislike who is gazing back at me?

————

I return to New York City frequently. I have friends to visit and work to do. One evening, I stood in Brooklyn Bridge Park staring up at the Gair Building. Its four illuminated clock faces shone like terrestrial moons over the East River.

It was six o'clock.

In that instant—the moment within a minute that comprises hours in a day that gather weeks into a year—I let time pass over me.

I felt the future bearing down.

Permission not granted

*Little Megan. Painting courtesy of
Thedra Cullar-Ledford.*

ACKNOWLEDGMENTS

To my family and my friend family: Now and forever.
Thank you, Mark Wunderlich, for your constant support and friendship. To Jenny Boully for believing in my work and encouraging me onward. I am forever grateful to Walter M. Robinson for your support and friendship. To Phillip Lopate for getting me started. To my Bennington teachers and mentors: Benjamin Anastas, Susan Cheever, Peter Trachtenberg, and Joan Wickersham. To Mary Gaitskill for your kindnesses. To the community of the Bennington Writing Seminars: you mean the world to me.

The Little Megan doll was a gift from my dear and talented friend Elizabeth Evitts Dickinson, from her mother's collection. The painting of the Little Megan doll is a gift from my friend and artist Thedra Cullar-Ledford. Thank you for lifting me up and keeping me laughing: Albert Abonado, Monica Adkins, J. Mae Barizo, Rebecca Boucher, Nicole Chung, Will Donnelly, Rebecca Donner, Matthew Groner, Frances Greathead, Haley Hach, Abby Hagler, James Tate Hill, Jay Hodges, Chelsea Hodson, Gabe Hudson, Taylor Larsen, Chin-Sun Lee, D. J. Lee, Eve MacNeill, Nancy Manter, Kelly Marages, Jennifer Mathy, Jill McCorkle, Deb Mell, Susan Merrell,

Suzanne Merritt, Jennifer Miller, Ander Monson, Rena J. Mosteirin, Titi Nguyen, Sara Diane Nolan, Jennifer Pastiloff, Joanne Proulx, Hugh Ryan, Erin Kate Ryan, Matt Salesses, Leigh Stein, Angelique Stevens, Clifford Thompson, Carly Willsie, V., and Nick Yetto.

My work has received support from The Saltonstall Foundation, which allowed me to find the Domecon babies and gave me time to play. Fellowships at The Virginia Center for the Creative Arts and The Horned Dorset Colony gave me much-needed space to write many of the essays in this book.

Thank you to Joy Castro and Kristen Elias Rowley at Mad Creek Books for hearing my voice and lifting me up from the slush pile. Thank you to the entire team at Ohio State University Press.

To all the adoptees out there: I see you.

PREVIOUS PUBLICATION ACKNOWLEDGMENTS

I am grateful to the wonderful editors at these fine journals for publishing my work:

"Hold Me Like a Baby": *Tupelo Quarterly* (2020), feature and interview.

"Confession": *Monkeybicycle* (2018). Nominated for a Pushcart Prize.

"Water:" *My Body My Words* anthology (2018). Edited by Amye Archer and Loren Kleinmen.

"Talking Points": *The Coachella Review* (2017). Nominated for a Pushcart Prize.

"Sin Will Find You Out": *Catapult* and *Longreads* (2016). Notable, *Best American Essays 2017.*

"Losing It": *(b)OINK* (2017).

"Learning to Mother Myself": *The Manifest Station* (2016). Jennifer Pastiloff and Angela Giles, editors.

"O' Father Where Art Thou": *Literary Orphans* Anthology (2015). *The Tishman Review.*

"Consider the Lilies": *Literary Orphans* (2015). Reprinted in *The Lost Daughters.*

"O' Father Where Art Thou": *Revolution John Magazine* (2015).

"What to Expect When You Least Expect It": *Drafthorse* (2015).

"Mother's Day": broadcast on *51% The Women's Perspective* WAMC-NPR (2011).

"The Dollhouse" artwork has appeared in the following exhibitions:

"Reliquary": Smallbany Gallery, Albany, NY (2020). Curated by Katherine Chwazik.

"Practice Babies": *What Is That Leaping Inside Your Chest?* Collar Works Gallery, Troy, NY (2018). Curated by Alexandra Foradas, assistant curator at MASS MoCA.

"Does This Tiara Make the Patriarchy Look Fat?" *Nasty Women of the North,* Collar Works Gallery, Troy, NY (2017). Organized by The Feminist Art Project of Upstate NY to benefit Planned Parenthood.

"The Dollhouse": Fence Select Show, Arts Center of the Capital Region, Troy, NY (2017). Juried by Michael Oatman.

"XXX Girly Show": Collected Charms, Group Show, Arts Center of the Capital Region, Troy, NY (2017).

MACHETE

Joy Castro, Series Editor

This series showcases fresh stories, innovative forms, and books that break new aesthetic ground in nonfiction—memoir, personal and lyric essay, literary journalism, cultural meditations, short shorts, hybrid essays, graphic pieces, and more—from authors whose writing has historically been marginalized, ignored, and passed over. The series is explicitly interested in not only ethnic and racial diversity, but also gender and sexual diversity, neurodiversity, physical diversity, religious diversity, cultural diversity, and diversity in all of its manifestations. The machete enables path-clearing; it hacks new trails and carves out new directions. The Machete series celebrates and shepherds unique new voices into publication, providing a platform for writers whose work intervenes in dangerous ways.

The Guild of the Infant Saviour: An Adopted Child's Memory Book
MEGAN CULHANE GALBRAITH

Like Love
MICHELE MORANO

Quite Mad: An American Pharma Memoir
SARAH FAWN MONTGOMERY

Apocalypse, Darling
BARRIE JEAN BORICH